D0835508

Fitba Gallimaufry

Fitba Gallimaufry

by Adam Scott

SPORTS
BOOKS

Published in Great Britain by
SportsBooks Limited
PO Box 422
Cheltenham
GL50 2YN
Tel: 01242 256755
Fax: 01242 254694
email: info@sportsbooks.ltd.uk
www.sportsbooks.ltd.uk

Cover designed by Alan Hunns.
alan@hunnsgraphics.demon.co.uk

A catalogue record for this book is available from
the British Library.

ISBN 1 899807 45 4

Printed by Cromwell Press

Fitba Gallimaufry
An Introduction

In mediaeval universities, the trivium, the Latin root of the word **trivia**, comprised the first three subjects taught: grammar, rhetoric and logic. The trivium was a precursor to the final four of the liberal arts, the quadrivium, comprising arithmetic, geometry, music and astronomy.

When they found time to play fitba is unclear.

Gallimaufry is a noun meaning a hotchpotch, a jumble or a confused medley. Pronounced **gall-uh-maw-free**, it has its origins in the French – as, according to legend, does the nickname of Clyde FC, The Bully Wee.

It is said that around the year 1900, a group of French businessmen, on a visit to Scotland, ended up at Shawfield for a league game against Rangers. The legend implies that fitba-starved Gallic types could often be found on the terraces of Scotland indulging their passion, sick to the back teeth, perhaps, of bicycle racing. During the match, the referee disallowed a perfectly legal Clyde goal. Incensed at the injustice, one of the French party cried out, "But il'y, oui?" – heard as "Bully wee" and translated as "Their goal, yes?".

The correct response to this tall tale is, of course, the Scots double-positive-that-makes-a-negative: "Aye, right".

But if you *want* to believe it, then you've come to the right book.

Adam Scott, London & Edinburgh 2006

With thanks to John Murphy, Pete Baikie, Billy Scott and Moray Hunter, without whom...

The Teams

"No one is bigger than the team".
Popular football sooth

I'll Say One Thing For...

Never again need you be marooned in pub conversation, with this handy know-one-fact-about-each-Scottish-team guide.

Aberdeen

In an international match against Northern Ireland at Windsor Park, Belfast, in 1983, six Dons donned the dark blue of Scotland: Jim Leighton, Doug Rougvie, Alex McLeish, Mark McGhee, Gordon Strachan and Peter Weir. Willie Miller was absent through injury.

Airdrie United

In 2004, Airdrie United became the first club founded in the 21st Century (the year 2002) to lift a Scottish trophy when they took the Scottish Division Two Championship.

Albion Rovers

Jock White is the only player capped for Scotland while playing for the Wee Rovers, in a 2-1 reverse against Wales at Cardiff on 4 February 1922. Ex-Rover Sam Malcolmson played for New Zealand against Scotland in the 1982 World Cup, the Kiwis losing 5-2.

Alloa Athletic

Perhaps seeking to make his fortune, Alloa's Wee Willie Crilley – who had scored 49 goals in the 1921/22 season – crossed the Atlantic to play for Brooklyn Wanderers. His arrival, however, coincided with the aftermath of the Wall Street Crash and, after scoring 7 goals in 14 games in the 1931 season, he eventually returned to Alloa.

Arbroath

A number of angry fans locked out of Gayfield for a cup tie against Celtic on 8 February 1975 prompted the *Sunday Post* front page headline: "Mob Stampedes at Arbroath Match".

Berwick Rangers

Berwick's best ever cup run came not in the Scottish Cup following their disposal of Rangers in 1967 (they fell to Hibs in the very next round) but in the League Cup of 1963/64. The Wee Rangers won their section (topping Montrose, Stenhousemuir, Forfar Athletic and Brechin City), beat St Johnstone in a play-off (6-4 on agg), saw off Stirling Albion in the quarter-final (6-5 on agg) only to be pulled up by Rangers at Hampden, losing 3-1.

Celtic

Tommy Gemmell is the only Scot to have scored in two European Cup finals – against Inter Milan in 1967 (winning 2-1) and against Feyenoord in 1970 (losing 2-1).

Clyde

Clyde were excluded from European football in 1967, despite finishing in third place in the league, one place behind Rangers. The European Fairs Cup – forerunner of the UEFA Cup – operated a strict one club per city rule, and the berths went to 4th-placed Aberdeen, 5th-placed Hibernian and 6th-placed Dundee.

Cowdenbeath

When the Blue Brazil lifted the Third Division Championship trophy at the end of 2005/06, led by manager Mixu Paatelainen, it was their first Championship trophy for 67 years. Their last – the Second Division title of 1938/39 – saw them elevated to Division One for only five games of the 1939/40 campaign before the competition was abandoned due to the outbreak of war.

Following the cessation of hostilities, Cowdenbeath were restored to the second level, and finished bottom in season 1946/47.

Dumbarton

The Sons were unsuccessful in an audacious bid to sign Johan Cruyff in the early 80s – the Dutch legend preferred the lucrative pastures of the NASL and the Washington Diplomats.

Dundee

Due to an unexpected thaw in Brussels, the Dundee players were unable to train on Anderlecht's pitch before their 1962/63 European Cup quarter-final meeting, instead using the cramped environs of a local tennis court. Dundee ran out 4-1 winners.

Dundee United

The Arabs waited 70 years (since their foundation in 1909 as Dundee Hibernian) before lifting their first major silverware – the Scottish League Cup of 1979/80, taken from Aberdeen 3-0 after a replay.

Dunfermline Athletic

Bent Martin, The Pars' Danish goalie in the 60s played at inside-forward during practice matches at training, believing that it gave him an insight into the minds of his opponents.

East Fife

East Fife scored the first Scottish Cup Final goal to be broadcast live on radio on 16 April 1927 – a header from Jock Wood on the two-minute mark. (Celtic went on to win the final by three goals to one.)

East Stirlingshire

In October 1974, Alex Ferguson, in his first managerial post, presided over East Stirlingshire's first home league win over local rivals Falkirk for 70 years.

Elgin City

Elgin City were the last Highland League side to make the quarter-finals of the Scottish Cup. In 1967/68 they went out 2-0 to Morton in the last eight having seen off League opposition in Forfar (3-1 in first round) and Arbroath (2-0 in second round).

Falkirk

The Bairns boss Alex Totten was the first manager to attend the Scottish Cup Final in full Highland dress. His side went down 1-0 to Kilmarnock at Hampden in 1997.

Forfar Athletic

Forfar Athletic twice held Rangers to draws in Cup contests: penalties had to separate the two by a margin of 6-5 in the League Cup of 1985/86, with a replay required to send Rangers through to the final of the Scottish Cup 3-1 after a 0-0 draw in 1981/82. None of the ties took place at Station Park, the League Cup tie being held at Dens Park and both the Scottish Cup semi-final and the replay at Hampden Park.

Greenock Morton

Article number two from the original constitution of Morton Football Club dating from 1874 stated that "all meetings in connection with the Club be conducted on temperance principles".

Gretna

Gretna's John O'Neill collected his fourth cup runners-up medal in the Scottish Cup Final of 2005/06 against Hearts. Prior to forcing the Edinburgh club all the way to penalties, O'Neill had collected beaten finalist medals with Hibernian and Dundee Utd in the Scottish Cup, and with St Johnstone in the League Cup.

Hamilton Academical

In March 1888 a report appeared in the local press as follows: "A rather peculiar incident happened at Hamilton.

The Match Secretary, who has acted in that capacity for several seasons, was made the recipient of a marriage present, which was of such a shabby nature that he gave it back, and resigned his post and his membership". Source: www.acciesfc.co.uk

Heart of Midlothian

The Gorgie club has won the Scottish Cup at four different grounds: Hampden Park, Glasgow, in 1891, 1956 and 2006; at Logie Green, Edinburgh, in 1896; at Ibrox Park, Glasgow, in 1901 and 1906; and at Celtic Park, Glasgow, in 1998.

Hibernian

No national newspapers covered Hibernian's first foray into the European Cup – as Britain's only representatives – in the first round, first leg of the inaugural competition in 1955/56. Hibs defeated Röt-Weiss Essen, Champions of Germany (a nation, in turn, that held the title of World Champions), in Essen by four goals to nil.

Inverness Caledonian Thistle

In 1994 Inverness Caledonian Thistle became the first Scottish club to be created by the merger of two existing clubs – Inverness Caledonian and Inverness Thistle – since Ayr FC and Ayr Parkhouse came together to found Ayr Utd in 1909.

Kilmarnock

It is thought that Kilmarnock's 2-0 reverse at the hands of Renton, played out on 18 October 1873, was the first game ever to be played in the Scottish Cup.

Livingston

Livingston – formerly Meadowbank Thistle and previously Ferranti Thistle – is the only British club to date to have employed the services of a Brazilian manager. Marcio Maximo served four months at the Almondvale helm during 2003.

Montrose

Montrose's finest giant-killing hour was a 3-1 aggregate defeat of Hibs in the quarter-final of the 1975/76 League Cup. They went on to lose the semi-final to eventual winners Rangers at Hampden in front of a crowd of 20,319 – a figure almost double the total number of souls that had witnessed their six group stage ties against East Fife, Raith Rovers and St Mirren.

Motherwell

In 1959 Ian St John scored a hat-trick for Motherwell against Hibs, completing his three-goal haul in two minutes and thirty seconds. On his debut for Liverpool he matched that tally but still ended up on the losing side – Liverpool went down 4-3 to Everton.

Partick Thistle

Alan Rough played in goal for Partick Thistle from 1970 to 1982. Voted Scottish Player of the Year in 1981, he played 53 times – including two World Cups, 1978 and 1982 – for Scotland, keeping 16 clean sheets.

Peterhead

The Blue Toon gained their first Scottish League promotion in 2004/05, making them the third of the four ex-Highland League clubs to climb out of the bottom division.

Queen of the South

Queen of the South's Palmerston Park was used as a helicopter landing pad for a visit to Dumfries by King Olaf of Norway in the 1960s.

Queen's Park

The Celts, The Northern and Morayshire were all proposed as names at the inaugural meeting of what would become Queen's Park – the name Queen's Park being carried by a meagre majority of one vote.

Raith Rovers

Raith were the most successful team in the history of the Penman Cup. An irregular tournament launched in 1905 for teams of the Lothians and Fife, it was expanded after WWI to include all east of Scotland teams. The Stark's Parkers won it a record six times.

Rangers

Anecdote has it that, when Moses and Peter McNeil founded the Rangers Football Club in 1872, the inaugural members soon decided that Peter was too old to play. This decision was rescinded when the elder McNeil threatened to withdraw the use of his football, the only one in the fledgling club's possession.

Ross County

Ross County's inaugural season in the Scottish League opened with a 2-0 win over Cowdenbeath on Saturday 13 August and closed on Saturday 13 May with a 2-3 reverse at East Stirlingshire. They finished 3rd in Division 3, three places above fellow ex-Highland Leaguers, the thrice-named Inverness Caledonian Thistle.

St Johnstone

The Saintees home ground – McDiarmid Park – is named after the local farmer, Bruce McDiarmid, who donated the land on which the stadium stands. It opened on 19 August 1989 and was Britain's first purpose-built all-seater stadium.

St Mirren

Former Buddy Iain Munro held the manager's job at Love Street for a mere 24 hours – from 9 to 10 September 1996 – before announcing that he would be unable to fulfil the post and leaving to take the helm at Raith Rovers, thus claiming the record for shortest managerial appointment in Scottish football history.

Stenhousemuir

Stanley Matthews once played for the Warriors, against local rivals Falkirk in a special fund-raising match during the 1955/56 season.

Stirling Albion

In the 25 years following their election to the League after WWII, the Binos were promoted on six occasions, and relegated an equal number of times.

Stranraer

Stranraer's Stair Park has three stands: the main stand, the Coo Shed stand and the bandstand situated in the public park that gives the ground its name.

~~~

Number of Seasons in Which the Old Firm Has Ended up Empty Handed: 2

	Champions	Scottish Cup	League Cup
1951-52	Hibernian	Motherwell	Dundee
1954-55	Aberdeen	Clyde	Hearts

~~~

Morton (now Greenock Morton) was the first Scottish club to become a limited company, doing so in 1896.

Longest Time Without a Trophy

Some of the longest gaps between trophy wins are....

Partick Thistle **50 years**
Scottish Cup 1921– League Cup 1971

Hearts **48 years**
Scottish Cup 1906 – League Cup 1954

Hibernian **45 years**
Championship 1903 – Championship 1948

Dundee **41 years**
Scottish Cup 1910 – League Cup 1951

Kilmarnock **36 years**
Scottish Cup 1929 – Championship 1965

St Mirren **28 years**
Scottish Cup 1959 – Scottish Cup 1987

Motherwell **18 years**
Championship 1932 – League Cup 1950

Clyde **16 years**
Scottish Cup 1939 – Scottish Cup 1955

Aberdeen **15 years**
League Cup 1955 – Scottish Cup 1970

Dundee Utd **11 years**
Championship 1983 – Scottish Cup 1994

East Fife **9 years**
Scottish Cup 1938 – League Cup 1947

Dumbarton **8 years**
Scottish Cup 1883 – Championship 1891

Rangers **8 years**
Scottish Cup 1903 – Championship 1911

Dunfermline Ath **7 years**
Scottish Cup 1961 – Scottish Cup 1968

Celtic **6 years**
Scottish Cup 1989 – Scottish Cup 1995

Queen's Park **4 years**
Scottish Cup 1876 – 1880, 1886 – 1890.

Last time they won anything the open-top bus was horse-drawn and the trophy was made of wood...

Supporters at the end of 2005/06 season that had waited more than two years since seeing their team lift a major trophy.

Dumbarton **114 years**	League Championship 1892
Queen's Park **113 years**	Scottish Cup 1893
Morton **84 years**	Scottish Cup 1922
East Fife **53 years**	League Cup 1953
Falkirk **49 years**	Scottish Cup 1957
Clyde **48 years**	Scottish Cup 1958
Dunfermline Ath **38 years**	Scottish Cup 1968
Partick Thistle **35 years**	League Cup 1971
Dundee **33 years**	League Cup 1973
St Mirren **19 years**	Scottish Cup 1987
Motherwell **15 years**	Scottish Cup 1991
Hibernian **15 Years**	League Cup 1991
Dundee Utd **12 years**	Scottish Cup 1994
Raith Rovers **12 years**	League Cup 1994
Aberdeen **11 years**	League Cup 1995
Kilmarnock **9 years**	Scottish Cup 1997
Livingston **2 years**	League Cup 2004

"Badges? We Don't Need No Stinkin' Badges"

The above quote from *The Treasure of Sierra Madre* is untrue in the case of Rangers, a club that requires not one, but two badges: the RFC crest on their royal blue jerseys, and the lion rampant/panelled football club crest with the "Aye Ready" motto.

≈

Ten sides made the cut for the inaugural Premier League in 1975/76. They (with managers and final position in brackets) were: Aberdeen (Jimmy Bonthrone/Ally MacLeod, 7th), Ayr Utd (Ally MacLeod/Alex Stuart, 6th), Celtic (Jock Stein, 2nd), Dundee (David White, 9th relegated) Dundee Utd (Jim McLean, 8th), Hearts (John Hagart, 5th), Hibernian (Eddie Turnbull, 3rd), Motherwell (Willie MacLean, 4th), Rangers (Jock Wallace, 1st) and St Johnstone (Jackie Stewart, 10th relegated).

≈

Make Mine The Double

The Double is the combination of winning the Scottish Championship and the Scottish Cup in one season. However, A Double, if not The Double, has been achieved on the following occasions:

1959/60	**Hearts**	League & League Cup
1960/61	**Rangers**	League & League Cup
1961/62	**Rangers**	Scottish Cup & League Cup
1965/66	**Celtic**	League & League Cup
1967/68	**Celtic**	League & League Cup
1969/70	**Celtic**	League & League Cup

1978/79	**Rangers**	Scottish Cup & League Cup
1985/86	**Aberdeen**	Scottish Cup & League Cup
1996/97	**Rangers**	League & League Cup
1997/98	**Celtic**	League & League Cup
2001/02	**Rangers**	Scottish Cup & League Cup
2005/06	**Celtic**	League & League Cup

≈≈≈

There are five senior Scottish sides whose names begin and end in the same letter. They are:

Celtic
Dundee Utd
East Fife
East Stirlingshire
Kilmarnock

≈≈≈

An Even Spread

Number of post-war seasons in which three sides have shared the three major trophies between them: 16.

	Champions	**Scottish Cup**	**League Cup**.
1947/48	Hibernian	Rangers	East Fife
1950/51	Hibernian	Celtic	Motherwell
1951/52	Hibernian	Motherwell	Dundee
1954/55	Aberdeen	Clyde	Hearts
1955/56	Rangers	Hearts	Aberdeen
1956/57	Rangers	Falkirk	Celtic
1957/58	Hearts	Clyde	Celtic
1958/59	Rangers	St Mirren	Hibernian
1964/65	Kilmarnock	Celtic	Rangers
1972/73	Celtic	Rangers	Hearts
1979/80	Aberdeen	Celtic	Dundee Utd

1980/81	Celtic	Rangers	Dundee Utd
1981/82	Celtic	Aberdeen	Rangers
1982/83	Dundee Utd	Aberdeen	Celtic
1984/85	Aberdeen	Celtic	Rangers
1994/95	Rangers	Celtic	Raith Rovers

One letter of the alphabet appears only once in the names of all the senior sides in Scotland and England. It is the letter 'J' of St Johnstone.

Some Club Crests

- Only one team in Scotland features a musical instrument on its club crest – Hibernian with a harp.
- Berwick Rangers wear two lions on their shirt – the lion rampant of Scotland and the lion passant of England.
- Four Scottish clubs feature sailing ships on their crests: Clyde, Greenock Morton, Hibernian and Stranraer.
- 14 of the 42 senior Scottish clubs thought it appropriate to include a football in the club's crest: Aberdeen, Brechin City, Cowdenbeath, East Fife, East Stirlingshire, Falkirk, Greenock Morton, Hearts, Hibernian, Kilmarnock, Montrose, Motherwell, Peterhead and Rangers.
- Thistles on their livery: Cowdenbeath, Inverness Caledonian Thistle, Livingston and Partick Thistle.
- Clubs with lions rampant on their livery: Berwick Rangers, Cowdenbeath, Dundee Utd, Livingston, Queen's Park and Rangers.
- Clubs with elephants on their livery: Dumbarton.
- Number of squirrels on Scottish senior club crests: 2 – both on Kilmarnock's crest.

≈≈≈

During the Second World War (1939 – 1945) only one bomb fell on the town of Stirling. It destroyed the home of King's Park Football Club, and the club was unable to carry on following the cessation of hostilities. Its place was taken by newly-formed Stirling Albion who were elected to Scottish Division 'C' for the 1946-47 season.

Too close for comfort

Dundee's two senior clubs famously reside in the same street, less than 200 yards apart. In season 1987/88, the Arabs made a mammoth near-1000 yard round trip to take on their dark blue rivals at Dens Park, with the Dees trekking to Tannadice on three reciprocal occasions. The unprecedented eight competitive meetings in one season panned out thus:

League Cup	Dundee 2	Dundee Utd 1	02/9/87
Scottish Cup	Dundee 0	Dundee Utd 0	12/3/88
Scottish Cup*	Dundee Utd 2	Dundee 2	15/3/88
Scottish Cup**	Dundee 0	Dundee Utd 3	28/3/88
Premier	Dundee Utd 1	Dundee 0	
Premier	Dundee 1	Dundee Utd 1	
Premier	Dundee 0	Dundee Utd 2	
Premier	Dundee Utd 1	Dundee 3	

*Replay,**Second Replay.

…making a mythical City of Dundee League (with two points for a win, the convention of the day) look like this:

	P	W	L	D	F	A	Pts
Dundee Utd	8	3	2	3	11	8	9
Dundee	8	2	3	3	8	11	7

≈

The first Scottish side to carry shirt sponsorship was Keith FC in the Highland League of 1976, sponsored by Chivas Regal. Hibernian was the first League side, with Bukta in 1978

Scottish Clubs Whose Names Reveal no Clue to the Outsider of the Town/City of their Origin...

Albion Rovers (Coatbridge)
Celtic*
Clyde (Cumbernauld, formerly Glasgow)
East Fife (Methil)
East Stirlingshire (Falkirk)
Hearts (Edinburgh)
Hibernian (Edinburgh)
Queen of the South (Dumfries)
Queen's Park (Glasgow)
Raith Rovers (Kirkcaldy)#
Partick Thistle (Glasgow)§
Rangers*
Ross County (Dingwall)
St Mirren (Paisley)
St Johnstone (Perth)

*The official name of the team often referred to as
Glasgow Celtic is Celtic Football and Athletic Club.
The official name of the team often referred to as
Glasgow Rangers is The Rangers Football Club.
#Raith Rovers play in Kirkcaldy. Interestingly, the
   neighbouring Fife Flyers ice hockey team also
   eschews the name of its hometown.
§Partick have not played in the burgh of Partick since
   1909. They now play in Maryhill.

As a Consequence, the Streets of the Following Towns are *Never* Danced in:

Those of Raith or Albion.

Teams Yet to Beat Rangers in a Competitive Match (to end 2005/06)

Airdrie United
Alloa
Brechin City
East Stirlingshire
Elgin City
Forfar
Gretna
Inverness Caledonian Thistle
Montrose
Peterhead
Ross County
Stranraer

Teams Yet to Beat Celtic in a Competitive Match
(to end 2005/06)

Airdrie United
Alloa
Berwick Rangers
Brechin City
East Stirlingshire
Elgin City
Forfar
Gretna
Livingston
Montrose
Peterhead
Ross County
Stenhousemuir
Stranraer

Teams Never to Have Lifted One of the Three Major Trophies (Championship, Scottish Cup, League Cup)

Albion Rovers
Alloa Athletic
Arbroath
Ayr United
Berwick Rangers
Brechin City
Cowdenbeath
East Stirlingshire
Elgin City
Forfar Athletic
Gretna
Hamilton Academical
Inverness Caledonian Thistle
Montrose
Peterhead
Queen of the South
Ross County
St Johnstone
Stenhousemuir
Stirling Albion
Stranraer

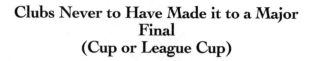

Clubs Never to Have Made it to a Major Final (Cup or League Cup)

Airdrie United
Alloa Athletic
Arbroath

Berwick Rangers
Brechin City
Cowdenbeath
East Stirlingshire
Elgin City
Forfar Athletic
Inverness Caledonian Thistle
Montrose
Peterhead
Queen of the South
Ross County
Stenhousemuir
Stirling Albion
Stranraer

~~~

Never a Dull Moment

Since its formation in 1874, Greenock Morton has been involved in more promotion (10 times) and relegation (12) campaigns than any other club. Add in to the mix two Scottish Cup finals (winner in 1922, runner-up in 1948) and one League Cup Final (runner-up in 1964), plus a jaunt to the 1968/69 Fairs Cup (ko'd first round 9-3 on agg to Chelsea), and the The Ton become, through sheer volume of meaningful involvement, Scotland's most exciting team to support outside of the Old Firm.

Booked

Some literary references in Scottish football.

Ayr United

The nickname of Ayr United, The Honest Men, can be found in the second stanza of the Robert Burns poem *Tam O'Shanter*: "Auld Ayr wham ne'er a toun surpasses/ For honest men and bonnie lassies.".

Heart of Midlothian

A local dance hall named after Sir Walter Scott's 1818 novel gave the Edinburgh side their name. The dance hall stood near the site of the notorious Heart of Midlothian gaol. In addition, famous Hibbie Irvine Welsh created Bruce Robertson, his protagonist of the novel *Filth* as a Hearts supporter.

Hibernian

Ian Rankin's 1998 novella *Death is Not the End* features a character named Stevie Scoular, wild boy striker with the Easter Road outfit. His long-running character from the Rebus series, Siobhan Clarke, is also a Hibbie.

Queen of the South

The Dumfries side are believed to have taken their name from the New Testament, Luke 11.31 "The queen of the south shall rise up in the judgement with the men of this generation, and condemn them."

Renton

Irvine Welsh was inspired by the name of the defunct Scottish club for the surname of his *Trainspotting* and *Porno* character Mark Renton.

~~~

The 1990s saw seven different sides lift the Scottish Cup: Aberdeen, Motherwell, Rangers, Dundee Utd, Celtic, Kilmarnock and Hearts.

East Fife 5 Forfar 4

This mythical tally, so beloved of English comedians, has yet to trouble either the scoreboard at Bayview or the classified results announcer at the BBC. The closest the teams have come in a competitive match is with the 1963/64 old Division Two fixture at Station Park which finished Forfar 5 East Fife 4 – a result that did not prevent Forfar from finishing second bottom of the table.

- The 1958/59 season was a vintage one for the pair, yielding the results Forfar 4 East Fife 4 and East Fife 4 Forfar 3.
- In 1960/61 the teams met three times (once in the League Cup) with the following results: East Fife 4 Forfar 3, East Fife 4 Forfar 2, Forfar 4 East Fife 1.
- Seemingly aware of the pursuit of the 5-4 Holy Grail, there have only been five no-scoring draws between the sides in 122 games and 85 years of competitive rivalry.

Forfar score four against East Fife – 12 occasions:
4-0 Div 2 1927/28, 4-1 Div 2 1935/36, 4-4 Div 2 1958/59, 4-1 Div 2 1960/61, 4-2 Div 2 1962/63, 4-3 League Cup 1964/65, 4-1 Div 2 1965/66, 4-2 1966/67, 4-1 Div 2 1969/70, 4-0 Div 2 1981/82, 4-1 Div 2 1982/83, 4-0 Div 1 1987/88.

East Fife score five against Forfar – 5 occasions:
5-2 Div 2 1929/30, 5-0 Div 2 1934/35, 5-3 Div 2 1937/38, 5-1 League Cup 1949/50, 5-2 Div 2 1964/65.

At the end of the 2005/06 season, the history of the fixture stood thus:

	Forfar Athletic wins	draws	East Fife wins
League	40	21	57
FA Cup	2	3	1
League Cup	1	0	7
Total	43	24	65

Some Scottish Club Origins

Amalgamation

The thought of amalgamation with a local rival is anathema to the modern fan. In the 19th and early 20th Centuries, however, it was the most common method of team-founding.

Aberdeen: From a merger of the Aberdeen, Victoria United and Orion clubs in 1903.

Albion Rovers: From the local clubs Albion and Rovers in 1882.

Brechin City: From a merger of Brechin Hearts and Brechin Harp in 1906.

Dundee: In 1893 from the local sides Our Boys and East End.

Elgin City: The amalgamation of Elgin Rovers and Vale of Lossie in 1893.

Breakaway

The founding of AFC Wimbledon is not without precedent.

Forfar Athletic: The members of the second-string side of Angus Athletic broke away in 1885 to found their own team, and outlived the older side.

Church

The original side of the Irish diaspora was born out of the church.

Hibernian: Formed by the young men of St Patrick's Church in Edinburgh's Cowgate in the year 1875.

Franchise

The practice of franchising – common in North American football and baseball – arrived on these shores in the late 20th Century.

Livingston: In 1995, Edinburgh's Meadowbank Thistle

was moved, lock stock and barrel, to the Scottish new town of Livingston.

Works

The explosion of football in a heavily industrialised west of Scotland in the 1870s and 1880s, brought about a proliferation of new sides.

Motherwell: Founded in 1886 from an amalgamation of two factory-based teams, Glencairn and Alpha.

Meadowbank Thistle: The team who became Livingston grew from the works team at Edinburgh's Ferranti plant.

Social

Amazing what boredom and a couple of pints of beer can inspire....

Dumbarton: Having witnessed Vale of Leven play Queen's Park, a group of local lads met at a Dumbarton hotel to found their own team.

Hearts: On the advice of a local bobby, who hated to see indolence on the street, a group of pals formed a team on The Meadows and named it after their favourite dance hall.

School

Hamilton Academicals: The team that does exactly what it says on the tin, FP's of Hamilton Academy founded Hamilton Academicals in 1874.

Other Sports

Rugby and cricket and their influence on the Scottish game....

Dunfermline: Seeking recreation and exercise in the winter months, the members of Dunfermline Cricket Club founded a football team in 1874. A similar story exists for St Mirren and, in England, Aston Villa.

Arbroath: A group of Arbroath rugby players challenged Dundee side St Clements to a match, and Arbroath FC was born in 1878.

East Stirlingshire: In 1880, Stirlingshire-based cricket club Bainsford Bluebonnets founded an offshoot football team called Bainsford Britannia – changing its name to East Stirlingshire the following year.

Broken Hearts

On the final day of the 1964/65 season, Hearts lost 2-0 to nearest title rivals Kilmarnock at Tynecastle allowing the Ayrshire side to draw level on points. Under the rules of the day, Kilmarnock won the Championship with a goal average superior by 0.04 goals

	P	W	D	L	F	A	Pts	G.Av
Kilmarnock	34	22	6	6	62	33	50	1.87
Hearts	34	22	6	6	90	49	50	1.83

The very next season, goal average was replaced by goal difference. Had the law been changed one year earlier, the League would have finished thus:

	P	W	D	L	F	A	Pts	G.Diff
Hearts	34	22	6	6	90	49	50	+41.
Kilmarnock	34	22	6	6	62	33	50	+29.

On the last day of the 1985/86 season, Hearts had to win or draw at Dundee to win the Flag. Two late Albert Kidd goals sank Hearts. Celtic's 5-0 victory over St Mirren allowed them to draw level on points and to overturn the goal difference of +2 in Hearts' favour. Celtic won the Championship.

	P	W	D	L	F	A	Pts	G.Diff
Celtic	36	20	10	6	67	38	50	+29.
Hearts	36	20	10	6	59	33	50	+26.

Had the rule of goal average still applied, Hearts would have won the League with a goal average superior by 0.02 goals.

	P	W	D	L	F	A	Pts	G.Av
Hearts	36	20	10	6	59	33	50	1.78.
Celtic	36	20	10	6	67	38	50	1.76.

Big Gate

Top home attendances of each club

Club	Gate	Opponents	Date
Rangers	118,567	Celtic	2/1/1939
Queen's Park	95,772	Rangers	18/1/11930
Celtic	92,000	Rangers	1/1/1938
Hibernian	65,860	Hearts	2/1/1950
Hearts	53,396	Rangers	13/2/1932
Clyde	52,000	Rangers	21/11/1908
Partick Thistle	49,838	Rangers	18/2/1922
St Mirren	47,438	Celtic	7/3/1925
Aberdeen	45,061	Hearts	13/3/1935
Dundee	43,024	Rangers	7/21953
Kilmarnock	35,995	Rangers	10/3/1962
Motherwell	35,632	Rangers	12/3/1952
Raith Rovers	31,306	Hearts	13/2/1954
St Johnstone	29,972	Dundee	10/2/1951
Hamilton Accies	28,690	Hearts	3/3/1937
Dundee Utd	28,000	Barcelona	16/11/1966
Dunfermline Ath	27,816	Celtic	30/4/1968
Albion Rovers	27,381	Rangers	8/2/1936
Stirling Albion	26,400	Celtic	11/3/1959
Cowdenbeath	25,586	Rangers	21/9/1949
Ayr United	25,225	Rangers	13/9/1969
Queen of the South	24,500	Hearts	23/2/1952
Morton	23,500	Celtic	29/4/1922
Falkirk	23,100	Celtic	21/2/1953
East Fife	22,515	Raith Rovers	2/1/1950
Dumbarton	18,001	Raith Rovers	2/3/1957
Arbroath	13,510	Rangers	23/2/1952
Berwick Rangers	13,365	Rangers	28/01/1967
Alloa Athletic	13,000	Dunfermline	26/2/1939
Stenhousemuir	12,500	East Fife	11/3/50

East Stirlingshire	11,500	Hibernian	10/2/1969
Forfar Athletic	10,800	Rangers	7/2/1970
Livingston	10,112	Rangers	27/10/2001
Montrose	8,983	Dundee	17/3/1973
Brechin City	8,122	Aberdeen	3/2/1973
Stranraer	6,500	Rangers	24/1/1948
Inverness CT	5,821	Dundee Utd	18/2/1998
Airdrie United	5.704	Morton	15/8/2004
Ross County	4,482	Inverness CT	12/2/1997
Gretna	2,307	Rochdale	16/11/1991
Peterhead	1,500	Fraserburgh	1999

≋

Teams Never to Have Been Relegated from the Top Flight

Aberdeen*
Celtic**
Inverness Caledonian Thistle#
Rangers**

*Elected to Division 1 1905/06.
**Founder members 1890/91.
#Elected to Division 3 1994/95.

Champions of the World

While the game was still in its infancy, a series of sporadic challenges were issued to contest the Football Championship of the World – usually between the Cup winning sides of Scotland and England. The results were as follows:

		Venue	**Date**
Hibernian 2	Preston NE 1	Edinburgh	13/8/1887
Renton 4	West Brom 1	Glasgow	19/5/1888
Spurs 0	Hearts 0	London	9/9/1901
Hearts 3	Spurs 1	Edinburgh	4/1/1902

≈≈≈

Hibernian and Rangers took part in the first six-figure transfer between two Scottish clubs. Colin Stein moved west in 1968 for £100,000.

≈≈≈

Some Team Liveries and their Origins

Dundee Utd

Played in tangerine strip as Dallas Tornado in the NASL during the close season of 1967. Manager Jerry Kerr was persuaded to adopt the colour by his wife, and the new livery had its debut against Everton in a pre-season friendly in 1969.

Hearts

Adopted maroon to echo the municipal livery of the Corporation of Edinburgh.

Hibernian

Adopted the green in tribute to the original players' Irish ancestry. Later copied by Celtic. The strip changed from dark green to emerald green with white sleeves in the 1930s in tribute to Herbert Chapman's Arsenal.

Liverpool

Scottish manager Bill Shankly added the famous red shorts in 1965 in an attempt to make his charges look bigger and more fierce.

Partick Thistle

Changed from dark blue to red and gold hoops when the West of Scotland rugby XV trained at Firhill in hooped shirts of those colours. The management, seeking to stand out from Rangers and Celtic, liked the look of the jerseys and adopted them soon after. In addition to having once reverted to the original dark blue, the Jags have also turned out in red and yellow stripes and red and yellow quarters.

≈≈≈

The motto of Queen's Park FC, still the only amateur club to play at senior level in the United Kingdom, is "Ludere Causa Ludendi": To play for playing's sake.

The Treble
Teams to have won all three major trophies

Aberdeen
Celtic
Dundee
Dundee Utd
Hearts
Hibernian
Motherwell
Rangers

... and Teams to have won them all in a single season

Celtic – three occasions 1966/67, 1968/69 & 2000/01.
Rangers – seven occasions 1948/49, 1963/64, 1975/76, 1977/78, 1992/93, 1998/99 & 2002/03.

≈≈≈

Shhhhhhhhhhh

At time of writing, Stenhousemuir FC has spent all but three seasons in Scottish League Division Two since its election to the league in 1922. Despite numerous reorganisations, The Warriors have remained at their numerical level whether that tier represents the second or third strata on the Scottish football roll of honour. In a comparatively frenetic burst of millennial activity, Stenny was first relegated from Division Two in 1998, bouncing straight back to their comfort zone the following season as Division Three runner-up.

Absent Friends

Whatever happened to the likely lads of the first League Championship 1890/91?

Cambuslang

This village side finished fourth in the inaugural League Championship. Finished bottom in season 1891/92 and did not seek re-election when Division Two was added.

Third Lanark

Declared bankrupt in 1967 and wound up in the same year – amid rumours of profiteering from the owner of the land upon which their Cathkin Park stood. Thirds finished fifth in the first League and went on to win it outright in 1904, adding a further Cup triumph in 1905 to their first win in 1889.

Abercorn

The Paisley side found itself unable to compete with local rivals St Mirren, and finally folded in 1920/21. Finished one position above St Mirren in the inaugural Championship in seventh place.

Vale of Leven

Veterans of seven Cup Finals – winning three – Vale ended in ninth place in 1891. Did not seek re-election for season 1892/93 following a victory-less second campaign. Joined Division Two in 1905 and played at that level until the outbreak of the First World War. After the Armistice, they resumed in Division Two in its first season back (1921/22) but were relegated to Division Three in 1924, going out of business with that ill-fated venture just two seasons later.

Cowlairs

Hailing from Springburn, Glasgow, Cowlairs FC was suspended from the second season of the League following allegations of professionalism. Played two seasons in Division Two from 1893 and folded in 1895.

Renton

The 11th XI in the inaugural League was expelled from the competition for playing against non-league opposition Edinburgh Saints. The Dunbartonshire village side was expelled a second time in 1887/88 (replaced by Hamilton Academicals). The former "World Champions" folded by the turn of the century.

- Port Glasgow Athletic, League members from 1893 – 1911 went by the most appropriate nickname of all the defunct sides: The Undertakers.
- Abercorn recorded the all-time lowest points tally with just 3 points in season 1896/97, with charity being found at Hibernian (2-2) and local derby rivals St Mirren (3-2).
- Northern, from Springburn in Glasgow, and Thistle (not to be confused with Partick Thistle) from the West of the same city boast the shortest league careers of all: one season, 1893/94, finishing second bottom and bottom respectively of the new Division Two.
- During their brief senior League sojourn, Port Glasgow Athletic took time out to dispatch the mighty Rangers from the Scottish Cup in 1905/06, 1-0 at the quarter-final stage.

Winning Big

Goal bonanzas, scoring frenzies and 36-goal thrillers – the record wins of the senior Scottish clubs.

Arbroath 36 Bon Accord 0 Scottish Cup 1st Round 1885

Stirling Albion 20 Selkirk 0 Scottish Cup 1st Round 1984/84

Elgin City 18 Brora Rangers 1 Highland League 1960

Peterhead 17 Fort William 0 Highland League 1998/99

Queen's Park 16 St Peter's 0 Scottish Cup 1st Round 1885/86*

Partick Thistle 16 Royal Albert 0 Scottish Cup 1st Round 1930/31

Hearts 15 King's Park 0 Scottish Cup 3rd Round 1937

St Mirren 15 Glasgow Uni 0 Scottish Cup 1st Round 1959/60

Hibernian 15 Peebles Rvrs 1 Scottish Cup 3rd Round 1961

Dundee Utd 14 Nithsdale W 0 Scottish Cup 1st Round 1931

Forfar Athletic 14 Linterdis 1 Scottish Cup 1st Round 1888/89

Aberdeen 13 Peterhead 0 Scottish Cup 3rd Round 1923

Rangers 13 Possilpark 0 Scottish Cup 1st Round 1877/88

St Johnstone 13 Tulloch 0 Scottish Cup 1887

Dumbarton 13 Kirkintilloch 1 Scottish Cup 1st Round 1888/89

East Fife 13 Edinburgh City 2 Division 2 1937/38

Montrose 12 Vale of Leithen 0 Scottish Cup 2nd Round 1974/75

Albion Rovers 12 Airdriehill 0 Scottish Cup 1887/88

Cowdenbeath 12 Johnstone 0 Scottish Cup 1st Round 1927/28

Motherwell 12 Dundee Utd 1 Division 2 1953/54

Brechin City 12 Thornhill 1 Scottish Cup 1st Round 1925/26

Celtic 11 Dundee 0 Division 1 1895

Ayr United 11 Dumbarton 0 League Cup 1952/53

Kilmarnock 11 Paisley Acad 1 Scottish Cup 1st Round 1929/30

Clyde 11 Cowdenbeath 1 Division 2 1951/52

Queen of the South 11 Stranraer 1 Scottish Cup 1st Round 1931/32

Greenock Morton 11 Carfin Shamrock 1 Scottish Cup 4th Round 1886/87

Falkirk 10 Breadalbane 0 Scottish Cup 3rd Round 1923 & 1926

Dunfermline Ath 11 Stenhousemuir 2 Division 2 1930/31

East Stirlingshire 11 Vale of Bannock 2 Scottish Cup 2nd Round 1888/89**

Raith Rovers 10 Coldstream 1 Scottish Cup 2nd Round 1953/54

Alloa Athletic 9 Selkirk 0 Scottish Cup 1st Round 2004/05

Dundee 10 Queen of the South 2 Division 1 1962/63#

Hamilton Acad 10 Cowdenbeath 2 Division 1 1932/33

Stenhousemuir 9 Dundee Utd 2 Division 2 1936/37

Inverness CT 8 Annan Athletic 1 Scottish Cup 3rd Round 1995/96

Berwick Rangers 8 Forfar Athletic 1 Division 2 1965/66§

Stranraer 7 Brechin City 0 Division 2 1964/65

Airdrie United 6 Berwick Rangers 0 Division 2 2003/04

Livingston 6 Aberdeen 1 League Cup 3rd Round 2001/02
*In the same round of the Cup as Arbroath 36 Bon Accord 0

**East Stirlingshire had dispatched Stenhousemuir 10-1 in the previous round – both matches won by a nine goal margin.

\# This victory was the second occasion on which Dundee had equalled their scoring record, with previous victories over Alloa Athletic and Dunfermline Athletic, both in 1947.

§ Berwick Rangers equalled their record victory the following season beating Vale of Leithen in the Scottish Cup.

Who do we hate around here?

Bitter rivalry stretches further than the enmity between the Old Firm sides. Those Scottish derby and grudge-match rivalries revealed in an easy ready reckoner for the outsider.

Angus Derbies
Arbroath v. Brechin City v. Forfar Athletic v. Montrose

Ayrshire Derby
Ayr United v. Kilmarnock

Dundee Derbies
Dundee v. Dundee Utd

Edinburgh Derby
Hearts v. Hibernian

Falkirk Derby
Falkirk v. East Stirlingshire

Fife Derbies
Cowdenbeath v. East Fife v. Dunfermline v. Raith Rovers

Glasgow Derbies
Celtic v. Clyde v. Partick Thistle v. Queen's Park v. Rangers

Highland Derbies
Aberdeen v. Elgin City v. Inverness Caledonian Thistle v. Peterhead v. Ross County

Lanarkshire Derbies
Airdrie United v. Albion Rovers v. Hamilton Academicals v. Motherwell

Lothian Derbies
Hearts v. Hibernian v. Livingston

"New Firm" Derby
Aberdeen v. Dundee Utd

Renfrewshire Derby
Morton v. St Mirren

Southern Derbies
Berwick Rangers v. Gretna v. Queen of the South v. Stranraer

Stirlingshire Derbies
Alloa Athletic v. Stirling Albion v. Stenhousemuir

Tayside Derbies
Dundee v. Dundee Utd v. St Johnstone

≈≈≈

Diamonds – and Bankies and Hi Hi's – are Forever

For the record: Honours and milestones of three recently
defunct Scottish Clubs.

Airdrieonians (1925-2001)
Scottish Cup Winners 1924
Scottish Cup Runner-up 1975, 1992 & 1995
European Cup Winners' Cup 1992/93 Round 1 v. Sparta Prague 1-3 on agg

Clydebank (1965 – 2001)
Second Division Champions 1975/76
First Division Runner-up 1976/77

Third Lanark (1872 – 1967)
Founder member of Scottish League
Champions 1903/04
Scottish Cup Winners 1889 & 1905
Scottish Cup Runner-up 1876, 1878, 1906 & 1936
League Cup Runner-up 1959/60

The Players

Chic Charnley to (then) Scotland boss
Andy Roxburgh:
Charnley: "Any chance o' a cap, Andy?".
Roxburgh: "How? Is the sun in your eyes?".

≈≈≈

Keeper's Ba!

- Scottish author and creator of Sherlock Holmes, Sir Arthur Conan Doyle helped to found Portsmouth AFC, and became their first goalkeeper.
- "Two Andy Gorams! There's only two Andy Gorams!" Opposing fans' chant to the Rangers 'keeper who had just been diagnosed with mild schizophrenia.
- Celtic's European Cup-winning goalkeeper Ronnie Simpson was the son of Jimmy Simpson, a professional footballer with Rangers.
- Celtic bought Simpson from Hibs in 1965. It had been Jock Stein's first act as Hibs manager to get rid of the goalie because he was too old.
- Aberdeen goalkeeper Marc de Clerc scored on his debut for the Dons in 1980.
- Former Arsenal and Scotland custodian Bob Wilson has the middle name of Primrose.
- Three Hibs goalies moonlighting in other sports: Andy Goram (1980s cricket), Oli Gottskalksson (1990s basketball), William Harper (1920s boxing).
- Frank Haffey, the Celtic goalie who conceded nine goals playing for Scotland against England at Wembley in 1961, later became a comedian and cabaret artiste.

- Ronnie Simpson kept goal for the Great Britain Olympic side of 1948.
- To rile Rangers supporters, Ayr United 'keeper Hugh Sproat would wear a green jersey. To similarly curry rancour with Celtic fans, he would switch his jersey to blue.

≈≈

The Many Clubs of Charles Callaghan Charnley

Chic Charnley began his football odyssey at amateur level with a side called **Possil Villa**. From here, he graduated to the juniors with **Glencairn**. Then, in 1982, aged just 19, he spent a year at **St Mirren** before being released by then new manager Alex Miller. A spell at **Ayr United** as a part-timer was followed by a period away from the game, working on the oil rigs. **Pollok Juniors** came next, a springboard to a start with **Clydebank** back in the senior game. Eighteen months later and it was off to John Lambie's **Hamilton Academicals**, then a Premier League outfit. Charnley followed Lambie to **Partick Thistle**, his first of four stints at Firhill*. A return to **St Mirren** came when then manager Davie Hay paid £250,000 for his services. A brief sojourn in England, on loan to **Bolton Wanderers** followed, and then it was off to the Swedish First Division with **Djurgårdens**. Charnley returned to Scotland in 1993, back to **Partick Thistle**#, a stay that was interrupted by a call from **Celtic**. A lifelong fan, Charnley played for the Hoops in a 3-1 victory over Manchester United in Mark Hughes's testimonial and was widely regarded to be the man of the match. Lou Macari, then Celtic manager, did not follow up on Charnley, and the Jags released the player on a free to **Dumbarton**. **Dundee** followed, with Dens manager Jim Duffy bringing the midfielder to **Hibernian** with his own move to Easter Road. Despite sparkling early season form in 1997/98, the clamour for his international call-up came to nought and with the arrival of Alex McLeish in Leith, it was back to **Partick Thistle** once more. A stint across the Irish Sea followed at **Portadown**, with Charnley taking up with **Kirkintilloch Rob Roy** in the Juniors upon his return. But on the 13 of September 2002 it was back to **Partick Thistle** for a fourth and final stay at the club with which he has become synonymous. He was 39 years old.

*Charnley signed his first Partick Thistle contract on April Fool's Day 1989.

It was in his second stint at Partick that Charnley famously fended off a training-session attack by a Samurai sword-wielding member of the public.

Rough Luck

In an interview with the *Topical Times Football Book* in 1976, Partick Thistle and Scotland goalkeeper Alan Rough detailed his myriad superstitious matchday rituals thus:

- No shaving for home matches.
- Take inventory of lucky charms: Partick Thistle key ring gifted by a fan on his debut; an old tennis ball; a miniature football boot "that I found in my goal one afternoon"; a little star-shaped medal.
- Always use the same dressing room peg: Number 13.
- Wear old-style Partick Thistle number 11 jersey beneath goalkeeper shirt.
- Bounce the ball three times off the tunnel wall before taking the field.
- Before kick-off, kick the ball into the empty net. "If I miss," Rough confessed, "I feel terrible for the rest of the afternoon.".
- During the match: "In my cap I keep a few handkerchiefs. Because I believe it's lucky for me to blow my nose as often as possible during a match."

As a footnote – a rabbit's footnote, if you will – Rough appeared on the BBC TV children's programme *Blue Peter* prior to the 1978 World Cup. The superstitious custodian was presented with a lucky charm to take to Argentina.

On Top o' the World, Ma

Two Scots played in the Rest of the World XI that lost 2-1 to England at Wembley 23 October 1963.

Jim Baxter (Rangers)

Denis Law (Manchester United)*

*Law scored the Rest of the World XI's goal. The side also included Ferenc Puskas and Alfredo de Stefano.

One Scot played in the POW XI that escaped to victory after taking on a Nazi XI in occupied Paris in the movie *Escape to Victory*.

John Wark (Ipswich Town)*

*Wark played Arthur Hayes of Scotland and wore the number 7 jersey.

NB The only player to have played in both England v. Rest of the World and Allied POW's v. Nazi Germany is Bobby Moore.

≋

The first Scottish player to score a goal in European football was Eddie Turnbull for Hibs against Rot Weiss Essen in Germany on 14 September 1955. The first European Cup goal scored on Scottish soil was from 21-year-old Jock Buchanan for Hibs in the return leg, a 1-1 draw on 12 October 1955. Buchanan was unable to take part in the following rounds as he was called up for National Service.

And the Winner Is...

Goalkeepers who have won the Scottish Football Writers' Player of the Year Award.

1967	Ronnie Simpson	Celtic
1974	David Harvey	Leeds Utd*
	Thompson Allan	Dundee*
	Jim Stewart	Kilmarnock*
1981	Alan Rough	Partick Thistle
1985	Hamish McAlpine	Dundee Utd
1993	Andy Goram	Rangers
2006	Craig Gordon	Hearts

*The 1974 Award was presented to the 22 players of the Scotland World Cup Squad, of which Harvey, Allan and Stewart were the goalkeepers.

Gordon Smith (1926 – 2006) won five Scottish League Championship medals with three different clubs – none of which were either of the Old Firm. They were Hibernian (1947/48, 1950/51 and 1951/52), Hearts (1959/60) and Dundee (1961/62).

Four Times Five...

Four strikers have notched up five goals in a Scottish Premier League fixture. They are:

Paul Sturrock	Dundee Utd 7 Morton 0	17 Nov 1984
Marco Negri	Rangers 5 Dundee Utd 1	23 August 1997
Kenny Miller	Rangers 7 St Mirren 1	4 Nov 2000
Kris Boyd	Kilmarnock 5 Dundee Utd 2	
		25 Sep 2004

Aff!

Legendary winger Willie Johnston was dismissed 21 times in his professional career.

Rangers 7 red cards
West Bromwich Albion 6 red cards
Vancouver Whitecaps 4 red cards
Hearts 3 red cards
Scotland 1 red card

~~~

Scots to Have Played in Serie A

Denis Law – Torino 1961 – 1962*
Joe Jordan – AC Milan and Verona 1981 – 1984
Graeme Souness – Sampdoria 1984 – 1986

*Law featured for the same Torino side as Joe Baker who, although transferred from Hibs and having been brought up in Motherwell, was ineligible to play for Scotland having been born in Liverpool. His nickname on England duty was "England's Scotsman".

The high street newsagent chain R.S McColl is descended from the small confectionary business set up by Queen's Park, Newcastle, Rangers and Scotland international centre-forward Robert Smyth McColl (1876-1959). The only professional to return to Queen's Park (where he reverted to amateur status), his career outside football earned him the nickname Toffee Bob.

Two Barney Battles! There's Only Two Barney Battles!

Bernard "Barney" Battles

Full-back/Wing-half

Born: Glasgow 13 January 1875. Died: February 1905

Capped three times for Scotland

Career: Hearts, Dundee, Celtic (where he won his caps) and Kilmarnock

was the father of…

Bernard "Barney" Battles

Centre-forward/Inside-right

Born: Musselburgh 1905. Died: November 1979

Capped once for Scotland and once for the USA

Career: Boston FC (USA) and Hearts (where he won his Scotland cap)

- Barney Junior was born after his father's death. Barney Senior succumbed to pneumonia at the age of just 30.
- Barney Senior won two Championships – one with Hearts in 1895 and one with Celtic in 1896 – in addition to two Scottish Cups with Celtic.
- Barney Junior scored three consecutive hat-tricks for Hearts in November 1930.
- Barney Senior was one of three players (with John Divers and Peter Meechan) to stage an impromptu strike in protest at the presence of two reporters in the press box for a match against Hibs in November 1896. Battles and the others had perceived insults in the scribes' coverage of an earlier match. Only two replacements were found (one being reserve Willie Maley) and Celtic played out a 1-1 draw with 10 men.
- In 1930/31 Barney Jr scored 44 goals in 35 League games for Hearts – still a club record.

Anglos

Some Scots internationalists who never kicked a ball in anger for a senior Scottish club*:

Arthur Albiston – to Manchester Utd in 1973 from schools football.

Matt Busby – to Manchester City in 1928 from Junior football.

Willie Donachie – to Manchester City in 1968 from Celtic ground staff.

George Graham – to Aston Villa in 1961 from schools football.

Asa Hartford – to West Bromwich Albion in 1966 from amateur football.

Denis Law – to Huddersfield in 1955 from schools football.

John Robertson – to Nottingham Forest from amateur football.

Bill Shankly – to Carlisle United from Junior football.

John Wark – to Ipswich Town in 1973 from schools football.

*Excluding wartime football when, for example, Matt Busby played with Hibernian.

≈≈≈

Of all the post-war English Division One sides, however, it was Leeds United that was the most eagle-eyed when it came to Scottish talent spotting:

Billy Bremner – to Leeds Utd in 1958 from Junior football.

Peter Lorimer – to Leeds Utd in 1962 from schools football.

Eddie Gray – to Leeds United in 1962 from schools football.

Jim McCalliog – to Leeds United as an amateur 1963 from schools football*.

David Harvey – to Leeds United in 1963 from schools football #.

Frank Gray – to Leeds United in 1970 from schools football.

*McCalliog did not play competitively for Leeds, but moved to Chelsea.

#Harvey was born in Leeds, but qualified as a Scottish international through his Scottish father.

The Gong Show

Kenny Dalglish is the most decorated Scottish footballer of all time, winning every major honour in Scotland and England.

Scottish League Championship medals: 4

Scottish Cup Winner's medals: 4

Scottish League Cup Winner's medal: 1

English League Championship medals: 7

FA Cup Winner's medal: 1*

English League Cup Winner's medals: 4

European Cup Winner's medals: 3

European Super Cup Winner's Medal: 1

As a manager, he won the Scottish League Cup once, the English title on four occasions and the FA Cup twice.

In addition, Dalglish:

- Won 102 Scotland caps between 1972 and 1986
- Scored 30 goals for Scotland, equalling Denis Law's record
- Was an inaugural inductee to the Scottish Football Hall of Fame
- Was an inaugural inductee to the English Football Hall of Fame
- Was nominated English Football Writers' Association Player of the Year 1979
- Named in Pelé's FIFA 100 in 2004 – the 125 greatest living players
- Is an MBE
- Is a Freeman of the City of Glasgow

*As player-manager

Ten One Club Men

Willie Bauld	Hearts	1946 – 1962
John Greig	Rangers	1961 – 1978
Billy McNeill	Celtic	1957 – 1975
Willie Miller	Aberdeen	1971 – 1990
Campbell Money	St Mirren	1978 – 1996
Lawrie Reilly	Hibernian	1945 – 1958
Alan Robertson	Kilmarnock	1972 – 1988
Doug Smith	Dundee Utd	1958 – 1976
Paul Sturrock	Dundee Utd	1973 – 1989
Joe Wark	Motherwell	1968 – 1984

≈≈

Gorgie no More.
Leith no More…

Some players who have crossed the Edinburgh divide
to play for both Hibernian and Hearts.

Hibernian 1941–1959 – **Gordon Smith** – Hearts
 1959–1961

Hearts 1962–1963 & 1967–1969 – **Willie Hamilton**
 – Hibernian 1963–1965

Hearts 1961–1969 – **Alan Gordon**
 – Hibernian 1972–1974

Hibernian 1967–1970 – **Peter Marinello** – Hearts
 1981–1983

Hibernian 1992–1997 – **Darren Jackson** – Hearts
 1999–2001

Hibernian 1998–2000 – **Paul Hartley** – Hearts –
 2003–time of writing

Hearts 2004–2005 – **Michael Stewart** – Hibernian
 2005–time of writing

Go West, Old Man

Following a low-key genesis in the late 60s, in which Aberdeen and Dundee Utd both played a part, the North American Soccer League – the NASL – exploded in a blast of 70s razzmatazz, capturing the imagination of every British schoolboy under the age of nine, and the wallet of every British pro over the age of 39. Pelé, Beckenbauer and Cruyff saw out their careers in the short lived set-up, along with the following disparate band of Scots….

Archie Gemmill (ex-St Mirren & Nottm Forest) **Jacksonville Teamen** 1982

Alfie Conn (ex-Rangers & Celtic) **San Jose Earthquakes** 1980

David Harvey (ex-Leeds Utd) **Vancouver Whitecaps** 1980–1982

Willie Johnston (ex-Rangers) **Vancouver Whitecaps** 1979– 982

Jimmy Gabriel (ex-Dundee & Everton) **Seattle Sounders** 1974–1976

Jim Holton (ex-Manchester Utd) **Miami Toros** 1976, **Detroit Express** 1981

Jimmy Johnstone (ex-Celtic) **San Jose Earthquakes** 1975

Don Masson (ex-QPR & Derby) **Minnesota Kick** 1981

Willie Morgan (ex-Manchester Utd) **Minnesota Kick** 1978–80

Willie Donachie (ex-Manchester City) **Portland Timbers** 1980– 982

Alex Cropley (ex-Hibernian) **Toronto Blizzard** 1980

Peter Lorimer (ex-Leeds Utd) **Toronto Blizzard** 1979– 1980 & **Vancouver Whitecaps** 1981–1983

Charlie Cooke (ex-Dundee & Chelsea) **LA Aztecs** 1976–1978

Scottish Footballing Brothers

- Brothers Jim and Tommy McLean contested the 1991 Scottish Cup Final as managers, with Tommy's Motherwell running out 4-3 winners over Dundee Utd. Their brother Willie had previously been Motherwell manager from 1975 – 1978.
- Gary and Steven Caldwell (of Hibernian and Sunderland respectively) played in the same Scotland XI against Switzerland in 2006.
- Brothers Bob and Bill Shankly led sides to League titles on both sides of the Tweed: Bob with Dundee in 1961/62 and Bill with Liverpool in 1963/64. The Shankly brothers then led their clubs to the European Cup semi-final in the subsequent seasons.
- Willie and Tommy Callaghan both played in the Dunfermline side which won the Scottish Cup in 1968, defeating Hearts 3-1 in the final. This feat was repeated by Paul and Willie McStay for Celtic in 1985 in beating Dundee Utd 2 – 1 after extra time.
- In February 2005, twin brothers Dick and Ian Campbell were each awarded manager-of-the-month awards – Dick with Partick Thistle in Division One and Ian with Brechin in Division Two.
- Ivano and Dario Bonetti were appointed manager and assistant manager of Dundee FC in May 2000.
- Dunfermline Athletic have fielded two sets of brothers in losing Cup Final sides – on both occasions the Pars going down to Celtic. Tommy and Willie Callaghan in 1965 and Derek and Darren Young in 2004.

George Best: Six Months in Headlines

At the end of 1979/80, Hibernian FC was relegated for the first time in 50 years: but not without first signing football legend George Best in a last-ditch attempt to stay up. If it failed in this, the move certainly succeeded in lighting up the pitches of Scotland whenever he played, and both the front and back pages whenever he didn't. The headlines all started with...

Answer for Hibs – buy George Best

in the *Edinburgh Evening News* on 5 November 1979. With Hibs adrift at the foot of the Premier Division, and Hearts by no means guaranteed a promotion spot from Division One, journalist Stewart Brown feared the prospect of a first ever season with no Capital involvement in the top flight. On 7 November, the *Daily Record* waded in with...

You're Joking, says George

in which Fulham boss Bobby Campbell claimed, "I spoke to George [about Hibs' bid] and he just laughed." Nevertheless, later that same day, the *Evening News* pressed on with.

Fulham OK Hibs bid to approach Best

and revealing, a week later...

BEST SAYS: I WANT TO PLAY FOR HIBS

a prelude to the simple front page splash of the 16th...

Best signs

not to be outdone, next morning's *Record* hailed...

MAC-BEST!

across its front page, cajoling the following from the legendary Irishman in an exclusive four days later:..

GOODBYE TO THE BIRDS AND THE BEVVY

"I'm off the bevvy," confided George, "I don't go to nightclubs and I'm not coming to Scotland to mess up again."

Fans all set for George's moment of truth

mused the *News* on the eve of his debut against St Mirren at Love Street. Such interest was generated that a local coach hire company representative boasted of booming business: "We've had enquiries from as far away as Hawick and Dunbar." George scored but the Saints ran out 2-1 winners. Against Partick in his home debut, before 20,622 (twice the gate of that day's League Cup semi at Hampden), the *Record* described Best's Leith bow as...

STORY BOOK STUFF

with Best orchestrating a 2-1 win. "Afterwards," noted the *Record* scribe, "(Best) sipped a glass of lager which he didn't even finish."

No real Mystery about Best's absence

assured the *News* a week later, following a no-show at Cappielow with Hibs' chairman Tom Hart providing the alibis. The whiff of scandal, however, was blown away with...

"A complete travesty"

An even bigger Bestie aberration? No, merely the *Record* expressing the general feeling that a George-inspired Hibs should have ran out more than mere 2-1 winners over Rangers just before Christmas. All was quiet on the Best front – save on the park where he featured in five Hibs wins (they had won only one before his arrival) – until...

Best Suspended

on the front page of the *Evening News*, following George's disappearance before a game against Morton.

Best apologises – ban is lifted

(in the *News*, again) seemed to put the affair to bed, before the festival of alliteration that was the *Daily Record* front page of 18 February 1980...

BAD BOY BEST SACKED BY HIBS

"Booze," it quoted the AWOL Irishman as saying, "has become my master."

Best's drinks spree costs him £40,000

added the *Evening News*. Best had gone on a three-day bender, culminating in a party at the North British hotel with the Scotland and France rugby teams. His Hibs career was over. Until, that is, he slipped back into the fold, announced in the *Evening News*...

Back... two of the Best

which saw the errant genius posing with newly appointed Hibs assistant Willie Ormond.

Best: I feel that I'm winning the battle

Unlike Hibs. Rooted to the bottom of the Premier League, manager Eddie Turnbull was sacked, with Ormond moving to the top job. Best treated Leith to one more virtuoso turn...

The Great Georgie Best Show

according to the *Evening News*, which hailed the "exquisite entertainment" and "bewildering skills" of the man in a 2-0 win over Dundee. But it was all over for Hibs and Best. Thanking the Hibs fans over the PA, the Irishman headed back to San Jose Earthquakes, taking his talents for football and headline-making with him, returning only for a brief spell the following season to play with Hibs in division one. He hadn't saved Hibs from relegation as Stewart Brown had predicted, but he had kept Brown and his colleagues in headlines and copy for six unique months.

Top Scorers of the Post-War Era

Top hitting marksmen from the old Division One, the Premier Division and the SPL.

1946/47	Robert Mitchell (Third Lanark)	22
1947/48	Archie Aikman (Falkirk)	20
1948/49	Alexander Stott (Dundee)	30
1949/50	Willie Bauld (Hearts)	30
1950/51	Lawrie Reilly (Hibernian)	22*
1951/52	Lawrie Reilly (Hibernian)	27*
1952/53	Lawrie Reilly (Hibernian)	30
	Charles Fleming (East Fife)	30
1953/54	Jimmy Wardhaugh (Hearts)	27
1954/55	Willie Bauld (Hearts)	21
1955/56	Jimmy Wardhaugh (Hearts)	28
1956/57	Hugh Baird (Airdrieonians)	33#
1957/58	Jimmy Wardhaugh (Hearts)	28*
	Jimmy Murray (Hearts)	28*
1958/59	Joe Baker (Hibernian)	25**
1959/60	Joe Baker (Hibernian)	42
1960/61	Alexander Harley (Third Lanark)	42
1961/62	Alan Gilzean (Dundee)	24*
1962/63	James Millar (Rangers)	27*
1963/64	Alan Gilzean (Dundee)	32
1964/65	Jim Forrest (Rangers)	30
1965/66	Joseph McBride (Celtic)	31*
	Alex Ferguson (Dunfermline Ath)	31
1966/67	Stevie Chalmers (Celtic)	21*
1967/68	Bobby Lennox (Celtic)	32*
1968/69	Kenneth Cameron (Dundee Utd)	26
1969/70	Colin Stein (Rangers)	24
1970/71	Harry Hood (Celtic)	22*
1971/72	Joe Harper (Aberdeen)	33
1972/73	Alan Gordon (Hibernian)	27
1973/74	John 'Dixie' Deans (Celtic)	26*

1974/75	Andy Gray (Dundee Utd)	20
	Willie Pettigrew (Motherwell)	20
1975/76	Kenny Dalglish (Celtic)	24
1976/77	Willie Pettigrew (Motherwell)	21
1977/78	Derek Johnstone (Rangers)	25*
1978/79	Andy Ritchie (Morton)	22
1979/80	Doug Somner (St Mirren)	25
1980/81	Frank McGarvey (Celtic)	23*
1981/82	George McCluskey (Celtic)	21*
1982/83	Charlie Nicholas (Celtic)	29
1983/84	Brian McClair (Celtic)	23
1984/85	Frank McDougall (Aberdeen)	22*
1985/86	Ally McCoist (Rangers)	24
1986/87	Brian McClair (Celtic)	35
1987/88	Tommy Coyne (Dundee)	33§
1988/89	Mark McGhee (Celtic)	16
	Charlie Nicholas (Aberdeen)	16
1989/90	John Robertson (Hearts)	17
1990/91	Tommy Coyne (Celtic)	18
1991/92	Ally McCoist (Rangers)	34*
1992/93	Ally McCoist (Rangers)	34*
1993/94	Mark Hateley (Rangers)	22*
1994/95	Tommy Coyne (Motherwell)	16
1995/96	Pierre van Hooijdonk (Celtic)	26##
1996/97	Jorge Cadete (Celtic)	25
1997/98	Marco Negri (Rangers)	32
1998/99	Henrik Larsson (Celtic)	29
1999/00	Mark Viduka (Celtic)	25
2000/01	Henrik Larsson (Celtic)	35*
2001/02	Henrik Larsson (Celtic)	29*
2002/03	Henrik Larsson (Celtic)	28
2003/04	Henrik Larsson (Celtic)	30*
2004/05	John Hartson (Celtic)	25
2005/06	Kris Boyd (Rangers)	32+

*Top scorer played for Champion team.
**First Englishman to lead scoring in the Scottish League.
Lowest ever finish for a team with the top scorer – Airdrieonians finished 11th.
First non-British player to top the scoring in the Scottish League.
§ Only player to top the scoring chart with three different teams.
+ Kris Boyd scored the first 15 goals of season 2005/06 with Kilmarnock.

≈≈≈

Archie Gemmill became the first official substitute in Scottish football when, playing for St Mirren, he came on for Jim Clunie in the League Cup match against Clyde at Shawfield, 13 August 1966.

≈≈≈

Before signing for Leeds United in 1958, Billy Bremner had been rejected by both Arsenal and Chelsea on the grounds that he was too small.

≈≈≈

The first Scots to win European winners' medals were Billy Brown and John White, with Tottenham Hotspur in the European Cup Winners' Cup final of 1963

The Cups

"You can just put that I am extremely disappointed by
the result. *Extremely* disappointed".

*Rangers' chairman John Lawrence to the waiting press pack
following the 1-0 defeat at the hands of Berwick Rangers in
1967*

≈≈≈

Giantkilling

• Celtic tumbled out of the Scottish Cup in Round
3 in 1999/2000, losing 3-1 at Celtic Park to Inverness
Caledonian Thistle (see chapter: The Old Firm).
• In 1986/87, Graeme Souness's Rangers lost 1-0 in
Round 3 of the Scottish Cup to Hamilton Academicals.
• In 2005/06 Celtic fell at their first hurdle losing
2-1 to Clyde in Round 3. The match was Roy Keane's
Celtic debut.
• In 1966/67 Berwick Rangers humbled their mighty
Glasgow namesakes with a 1-0 reverse at Shielfield
Park in Round 1 (see chapter: The Old Firm)

≈≈≈

Scottish Cup Final Hat-Tricks

John Smith Dumbarton 1881.
Jimmy Quinn Celtic 1904.
John 'Dixie' Deans Celtic 1972.
Gordon Durie Rangers 1996.

Aff!#2

Players red-carded in a Scottish Cup Final.

Jock Buchannan	Rangers	1929
Roy Aitken	Celtic	1984*
Walter Kidd	Hearts	1986*
Paul Hartley	Hearts	2006**

*Aitken and Kidd were captains of their respective teams.

**Hartley is the only man of the four to be dismissed from a winning side.

~~~

Scottish Cup All-Time Record

Wins		Runner-up
33	Celtic	19
31	Rangers	18
10	Queen's Park	2
7	Hearts	5
7	Aberdeen	8
3	Clyde	3
3	St Mirren	3
3	Kilmarnock	5
2	Hibernian	9
2	Falkirk	1
2	Dunfermline Athletic	2
2	Motherwell	4
1	Dundee Utd	7
1	Dumbarton	5
1	Dundee	4
1	East Fife	2
1	Greenock Morton	1
1	Partick Thistle	-
-	Hamilton Academicals	2

| - | Albion Rovers | 1 |
| - | Raith Rovers | 1 |

5 Number of defunct clubs to have won the Scottish Cup: Vale of Leven (1877, 1878, 1879), Renton (1885, 1888), Third Lanark (1889, 1905), St Bernard's (1895) and Airdrieonians (1924).

≈≈≈

North East Men Feared Drowned in Goals Bonanza

As every schoolboy knows, the highest ever score in a first class football match was when Arbroath squeaked past Bon Accord 36-0.

- The match was in the First Round of the Scottish Cup of 1885/86.
- On the same day, Dundee Harp battered Aberdeen Rovers 35-0.
- Dundee Harp captain Tom O'Kane, an ex-Arbroath man, wired his former club gloating of his new side's goal scoring achievements, unaware of how events had unfolded in Arbroath.
- In the Harp v. Rovers encounter, the referee counted 37 goals. The secretary of Dundee Harp, however, counted a mere 35. The lower tally was agreed upon, the referee admitting that it had been rather difficult for him to keep up with the scoring.
- Reduced to a mere spectator, legend has it that Arbroath goalie Jim Milne borrowed an umbrella from a friend in the crowd to keep dry during play.
- 15 Goal tally at half-time.
- 13 Top individual goal tally, going to John "Jocky" Petrie.
- 7 Number of Arbroath goals disallowed by the referee.

- 1 Number of lines in *The Scotsman*'s match report the following day.
- Third highest score in the same round: Queen's Park 16 St Peter's 0.
- Fourth highest score: Kirkintilloch Athletic 0 Renton 15.
- Next highest score: Alpha 6 Cambuslang Hibernians 8.
- At the same stage of the tournament in the following season, Arbroath banged 20 goals past Orion, another Aberdeen side.
- In a rematch with Orion the following season again – 1887/88 – and at the same stage of the tournament, Arbroath slipped up, managing only 18 goals to no reply.

The Arbroath side of the 36-0 victory:

Jim Milne (Snr), Bill Collie, Tom Salmond, Hen Rennie, Jim Milne (Jnr), Dyken Bruce, John Petrie, Johnny Tackett, Jim Marshall, David Crawford, Jim Buick.

- 9 Number of goals scored by Arbroath in Round Two, seeing off Forfar Athletic 9-1.
- 7 Number of goals scored by Arbroath in Round Three – Arbroath 7 Dundee East End 1.
- 3 Number of goals scored by Arbroath in Round Four, the stage at which they went out of the competition 5-3 to Hibernian.
- 4 Number of seasons since 1885 in which Arbroath have scored fewer than 36 goals in an entire season (Old Div One 74/75, Div Two 84/85, Div Three 96/97, Div One 2002/03).

Arbroath FC defeated Rangers at the very first time of asking, in the Scottish Cup of 1884, 4-3 at Gayfield. The Glasgow side, however, complained that the Arbroath pitch had not been wide enough. A replay was duly ordered, Rangers running out 8-1 victors.

"The Scots are a disputatious people"

(Willie Ross, later Baron Ross of Marnock,
Labour politician 1911 – 1988).

The footnotes at the bottom of any list of Scottish Cup Final results reveal a penchant for handbags, huffs and fisticuffs unrivalled in world football….

1879 Vale of Leven 1 Rangers 1
Footnote: Vale of Leven awarded cup, Rangers did not appear for replay.
The Story: Having been given a bye in the semi-final, Rangers took a 1-0 lead through William Struthers in the final. Struthers then had a goal disallowed for offside – a judgement that he and Rangers hotly disputed. Vale stole a soft equaliser in the 88th minute and Rangers boycotted the replay in protest.

1881 Queen's Park 3 Dumbarton 1
Footnote: After Dumbarton protested the first game, won 2-1 by Queen's Park.
The Story: "No fair!" cried the Sons of Dumbarton after a 2-1 reverse at the hands of The Spiders in the initial final, protesting at a number of spectators who had invaded the playing area. "Nae bother," replied the ever-gentlemanly Corinthians, "let's play again.".

1884 Queen's Park w/o Vale Of Leven dna.
Footnote: Queen's Park awarded cup, Vale Of Leven failed to appear.
The Story: Vale had two players out sick and one other with a family bereavement. The SFA, however, denied their request for a postponement and, in protest, Vale stayed home.

1889 Third Lanark 2 Celtic 1.

Footnote: Replayed by order of SFA due to playing conditions in the first match won 3-0 by Third Lanark.

The story: A snowstorm accompanied the Hi Hi's goalstorm and, although Thirds tried to claim the cup as theirs, the SFA declared the game "unofficial" and ordered a replay.

1892 Celtic 5 Queen's Park 1.

Footnote: After mutually protested game won 1-0 by Celtic.

The Story: 40,000 souls turned up to witness the first match and, after a series of pitch invasions, both captains informed the referee that they would be seeking a replay. The game was played out as a friendly, Celtic winning 1-0. The admission price was doubled to two shillings for the replay, and the crowd was reduced to 23,000. The defeated Queen's Park XI joined Celtic in a Glasgow hotel to celebrate.

1909 Celtic 2 Rangers 2. Celtic 1 Rangers 1.

Footnote: Cup withheld due to riot.

The Story: Some newspapers had suggested that there would be extra time after a second replay. None was played. Suspecting greed on behalf of both clubs, fans expecting to have to cough up for another game staged a protest that escalated into a riot, with the Hampden pay boxes being burned down. In an attempt to distance themselves from the riot and the allegations of opportunism, both clubs refused to play a third game, although neither would scratch. The SFA withheld the cup.

First Round of the First Scottish FA Cup 1873/74

Alexandria Athletic 2 Callander 0
Clydesdale 6 Granville 0
Dumbarton*– Vale of Leven –
Eastern 4 Rovers 0
Queen's Park 7 Dumbreck 0
Renton 2 Kilmarnock 0
Third Lanark*– Southern –
Western 0 Blythwood 1
*Dumbarton and Third Lanark given a walkover into the quarter-final.

~~~

- At time of writing, Hibernian have endured a cup-less drought stretching back 105 years to 1902.
- The only captain ever to lift both the Scottish and FA Cups has been Martin Buchan of Aberdeen (1970) and Manchester United (1977).
- The Scottish Cup is the oldest trophy in world football: The FA Cup predates the Scottish version by some two years, but the original FA Cup trophy was stolen in 1895.

5 Longest period in years without an Old Firm victory in the Scottish Cup Final, 1955 – 1959 (Winners: Clyde, Hearts, Falkirk, Clyde, St Mirren).

1955	Clyde 1 Celtic 0*
1956	Hearts 3 Celtic 1
1957	Falkirk 2 Kilmarnock 1*
1958	Clyde 1 Hibernian 0
1959	St Mirren 3 Aberdeen 1

*After a replay.

Tears in the Accounts Dept at the SFA Scottish Cup Finals Without Old Firm Involvement...

1874	Queen's Park 2 Clydesdale 0
1875	Queen's Park 3 Renton 0
1876	Queen's Park 2 Third Lanark 0*
1878	Vale Of Leven 1 Third Lanark 0
1880	Queen's Park 3 Thornliebank 0
1881	Queen's Park 3 Dumbarton 1
1882	Queen's Park 4 Dumbarton 1*
1883	Dumbarton 2 Vale of Leven 1*
1884	Queen's Park w/o Vale of Leven dna
1885	Renton 3 Vale of Leven 1*
1886	Queen's Park 3 Renton 1
1887	Hibernian 2 Dumbarton 1
1888	Renton 6 Cambuslang 1
1890	Queen's Park 2 Vale of Leven 1*
1891	Hearts 1 Dumbarton 0
1895	St Bernard's 2 Renton 1
1896	Hearts 3 Hibernian 1
1906	Hearts 1 Third Lanark 0
1910	Dundee 2 Clyde 1#
1913	Falkirk 2 Raith Rovers 0
1920	Kilmarnock 3 Albion Rovers 2
1924	Airdrieonians 2 Hibernian 0
1938	East Fife 4 Kilmarnock 2**
1939	Clyde 4 Motherwell 0
1947	Aberdeen 2 Hibernian 1
1952	Motherwell 4 Dundee 0
1957	Falkirk 2 Kilmarnock 1*
1958	Clyde 1 Hibernian 0
1959	St Mirren 3 Aberdeen 1

1968	Dunfermline Ath 3 Hearts 1
1986	Aberdeen 3 Hearts 0
1987	St Mirren 1 Dundee Utd 0##
1991	Motherwell 4 Dundee Utd 3##
1997	Kilmarnock 1 Falkirk 0
2006	Hearts 1 Gretna 1¶

*After a replay.

After two replays.

**After extra time in the replay.

After extra time.

¶ Hearts won on penalties.

21 Number of years Rangers had to wait before their first Scottish Cup Victory.

11 Number in years of longest period of Old Firm domination, 1971 – 1981, Celtic 6 wins, Rangers 5 wins.

- Despite Gretna's run to the Cup Final of 2006, East Fife hold the record for lowest League finish of all cup finalists, ending 5th in Division 2 – 25th place in Scotland – in 1926/27. (Gretna finished 23rd in the order of merit in 2005/06.).

- Of all Cup winners, it has taken Dundee Utd the longest to win the trophy: they first entered the Cup in 1924, losing in seven finals before finally lifting the trophy 1-0 against Rangers in 1994, 70 years after being knocked out 1-0 in the first round by Hibernian.

David v. Goliath

Scottish Cup Finals contested by teams not competing in the same Division of the League.

1892	Celtic (Div 1) 5 Queen's Park (Non-League) 1*
1893	Queen's Park (Non-League) 2 Celtic (Div 1) 1
1895	Saint Bernard's (Div 1) 2 Renton (Div 2) 1
1897	Rangers (Div 1) 5 Dumbarton (Div 2) 1
1898	Rangers (Div 1) 2 Kilmarnock (Div 2) 0
1900	Celtic (Div 1) 4 Queen's Park (Non-League) 3
1927	Celtic (Div 1) 3 East Fife (Div 2) 1
1938	East Fife (Div 2) 1 Kilmarnock (Div 1) 1
Replay	East Fife (Div 2) 4 Kilmarnock (Div 1) 2
1995	Celtic (SPL) 1 Airdrieonians (Div 1) 0
1997	Kilmarnock (SPL) 1 Falkirk (Div 1) 0
2006	Hearts (SPL) 1 Gretna (Div 2#) 1¶

*After a replay. First match declared void after mutual protest. See also section "The Scots are a Disputatious People"

In the case of Gretna, Div 2 = the third tier of Scottish football

¶ Hearts won on penalties

League Cup Final Hat-Tricks

Davie Duncan – East Fife 1947/48
Willie Bauld – Hearts 1954/55
Billy McPhail – Celtic 1957/58
Jim Forrest – Rangers 1963/64*
Bobby Lennox – Celtic 1968/69
John 'Dixie' Deans – Celtic 1974/75
Joe Harper – Hibernian 1974/75**
Ally McCoist – Rangers 1983/84
Henrik Larsson – Celtic 2000/01

*Jim Forrest scored four goals in total
**Joe Harper's hat-trick was scored for the losing side,
Hibernian going down 6-3 to Celtic

≈

The Complete League Cup Record

Wins		Runner-up
24	Rangers	6
13	Celtic	13
5	Aberdeen	7
4	Hearts	2
3	East Fife	0
3	Dundee	3
2	Dundee Utd	3
2	Hibernian	6
1	Motherwell	2
1	Partick Thistle	3
1	Raith Rovers	1
1	Livingston	0
0	Kilmarnock	4
0	Dunfermline	3
0	St Johnstone	2
0	Falkirk	1
0	St Mirren	1

0	Ayr Utd	1
0	Greenock Morton	1
0	Third Lanark	1

- Most final appearances without a win: 4 Kilmarnock 1952/53, 1960/61 1962/63 and 2000/01.
- Longest wait between final wins: 19 years, Hibernian 1972/73 – 1991/92.
- The largest margin of victory in a senior British cup final remains six goals – Celtic's 1957 League Cup win over Rangers by 7-1. This final broke the longest period without the Old Firm meeting in a major cup final – 29 years. Thanks to the non-removal of a lens-cap from a BBC camera after half time in the above match, no complete televisual record exists of the final.
- The 1980/81 League Cup Final – a local derby between Dundee and Dundee Utd – was staged away from Hampden Park, Glasgow. It was held at Dundee's home ground Dens Park, decided on the toss of a coin. United ran out 3-0 winners.
- Dennis McQuade, scorer of Partick Thistle's 3rd goal against Celtic in the 1971 League Cup Final was, at the time of the match, a student at Glasgow University.
- Jimmy Bone, scorer of Partick Thistle's 4th goal against Celtic in the 1971 League Cup Final, was, at the time of the match, a miner at Fallin near Stirling.
- Between 1964/65 and 1977/78, Celtic went on an unbroken run of 14 consecutive League Cup Finals, winning six.
- Longest period without Old Firm win: seven seasons 1949/50 – 1955/56 (winners East Fife, Motherwell, Dundee, Dundee, East Fife, Hearts and Aberdeen).

- From 1979 – 1981 the competition was known as the Bell's League Cup.
- From 1984 – 1993 the competition was known as the Skol Cup.
- From 1994 – 1998 the competition was known as the Coca-Cola Cup.
- From 1999 the competition has been known as the CIS Insurance Cup.

≈≈

Clap-the-Polis-Horse League Cup Finals

Known as Clap the Polis Horse Finals because of the lack of Old Firm involvement, the implication being that the fans of smaller teams, unused to the novelty of mounted police at a football match, can be seen outside Hampden patting the horses and chatting to the constabulary. See also the clichés "Family Final" and "It's a real family day".

1947-48	East Fife 4 Falkirk 1*
1949-50	East Fife 3 Dunfermline Ath 0
1950-51	Motherwell 3 Hibernian 0
1952-53	Dundee 2 Kilmarnock 0
1953-54	East Fife 3 Partick Thistle 2
1954-55	Hearts 4 Motherwell 2
1955-56	Aberdeen 2 St Mirren 1
1958-59	Hearts 5 Partick Thistle 1
1959-60	Hearts 2 Third Lanark 1
1962-63	Hearts 1 Kilmarnock 0
1979-80	Dundee Utd 3 Aberdeen 0*
1980-81	Dundee Utd 3 Dundee 0
1985-86	Aberdeen 3 Hibernian 0
1991-92	Hibernian 2 Dunfermline Ath 0
1995-96	Aberdeen 2 Dundee 0
2003-04	Livingston 2 Hibernian 0

*After a replay

Dundee Utd fans have yet to see their side lift the League Cup outside of their home town. Their two wins – 1979/80 and 1980/81 – took place at Dens Park, Dundee

≈≈≈

The League Cup by Numbers...

In the 60 tournaments from 1946 ...

...**12** sides have won the League Cup: Aberdeen, Celtic, Dundee, Dundee Utd, East Fife, Hearts, Hibernian, Livingston, Motherwell, Partick Thistle, Raith Rovers and Rangers.

...for two of them, it is the only major trophy the team has ever lifted: Raith Rovers (1994/95) and Livingston (2003/04).

Celtic made the League Cup final in every season of Jock Stein's reign as manager, contesting **13** finals, winning **6** of them, including **5**-in-a-row 1965/66 – 1969/70.

1 the number of major domestic trophies lifted by Ally MacLeod as manager (Aberdeen's League Cup win in season 1976/77 beating Celtic 2-1 AET).

8 east coast sides have lifted the trophy to only **4** from the west of Scotland.

≈≈≈

Local derbies in League Cup Finals

East Fife v. Dunfermline, Celtic v. Partick Thistle (twice), Celtic v. Rangers (12 times) and Dundee Utd v. Dundee.

The Leagues

Barber: "Anything off the top, Mr Shankly?"
Bill Shankly: "Aye. Everton."
*Apocryphal exchange between Bill Shankly and his barber in
the close season before Liverpool won the League, taking the
title from Everton 1963/64.*

Bottoms Up

At last, a list of last-place finishes

1890/91*	Cowlairs
1891/92	Vale of Leven
1892/93	Clyde
1893/94**	Thistle
1894/95	Cowlairs
1895/96	Linthouse
1896/97	Dumbarton
1897/98	Motherwell
1898/99	Abercorn
1899/00	Linthouse
1900/01	Motherwell
1901/02	Clyde
1902/03	Clyde
1903/04	Ayr Parkhouse
1904/05	St Bernard's
1905/06	East Stirlingshire
1906/07	Ayr Parkhouse
1907/08	Cowdenbeath
1908/09	Arthurlie
1909/10	Ayr Parkhouse
1910/11	Vale of Leven
1911/12	Albion Rovers
1912/13	Leith Athletic
1913/14	Johnstone

1914/15	Vale of Leven
1915/16#	Raith Rovers
1916/17	Aberdeen
1917/18	Ayr United
1918/19	Hibernian
1919/20##	Albion Rovers
1920/21	St Mirren
1921/22§	Clackmannan
1922/23	Arbroath
1923/24§§	Brechin City
1924/25	Montrose
1925/26	Galston
1926/27¶	Nithsdale Wanderers
1927/28	Armadale
1928/29	Armadale
1929/30	Brechin City
1930/31	Bo'ness
1931/32	Edinburgh City
1932/33	Edinburgh City
1933/34	Edinburgh City
1934/35	Edinburgh City
1935/36	Dumbarton
1936/37	Edinburgh City
1937/38	Brechin City
1938/39	Edinburgh City
1946/47¶¶	Edinburgh City
1947/48	Raith Rovers Reserves
1948/49	Edinburgh City
1949/50+	Alloa Athletic
1950/51	Alloa Athletic
1951/52	Arbroath
1952/53	Albion Rovers
1953/54	Dumbarton
1954/55	Brechin City
1955/56	Montrose

1956/57	East Stirlingshire
1957/58	Berwick Rangers
1958/59	Montrose
1959/60	Cowdenbeath
1960/61	Morton.
1961/62	Brechin City
1962/63	Brechin City
1963/64	Stirling Albion
1964/65	Brechin City
1965/66	Forfar Athletic
1966/67	Brechin City
1967/68	Stenhousemuir
1968/69	Stenhousemuir
1969/70	Hamilton Academicals
1970/71	Brechin City
1971/72	Hamilton Academicals
1972/73	Brechin City
1973/74	Brechin City
1974/75	Forfar Athletic
1975/76++	Meadowbank Thistle
1976/77	Forfar Athletic
1977/78	Brechin City
1978/79	Meadowbank Thistle
1979/80	Alloa Athletic
1980/81	Stranraer
1981/82	Stranraer
1982/83	Montrose
1983/84	Albion Rovers
1984/85	Arbroath
1985/86	Stranraer
1986/87	Berwick Rangers
1987/88	Stranraer
1988/89	Stenhousemuir
1989/90	East Stirlingshire

1990/91	Arbroath
1991/92	Albion Rovers
1992/93	Albion Rovers
1993/94	Cowdenbeath
1994/95ß	Albion Rovers
1995/96	Albion Rovers
1996/97	Arbroath
1997/98	Dumbarton
1998/99	Montrose
1999/00	Albion Rovers
2000/01	Elgin City
2001/02	Queen's Park
2002/03	East Stirlingshire
2003/04	East Stirlingshire
2004/05	East Stirlingshire
2005/06	East Stirlingshire

*Bottom of Division 1 (Single tier, only one division).

**Bottom of Division 2 (Second tier) 1893/94 to 1914/15.

\# Bottom of Division 1 (Single tier wartime league of 20 teams) 1915/16 to 1918/19.

\#\# Bottom of Division 1 (Single tier, expanded to 22 teams) 1919/20 to 1920/21.

§ Bottom of Division 2 (Second tier) 1921/22 to 1922/23.

§§ Bottom of Division 3 (Third tier) 1923/24 to 1925/26.

¶ Bottom of Division 2 (Second tier) 1926/27 to 1938/39.

¶¶ Bottom of Division 'C' (Third tier) 1946/47 to 1948/49.

+ Bottom of Division 2 (2nd tier) 1949/50 to 1974/75.

++ Bottom of Division 2 (3rd tier) 1975/76 to 1993/94.

ß Bottom of Division 3 (4th tier) 1994/95 to present day.

The Highland League

- Inverness sides took the first 19 Highland League Championships between 1894 and 1912: Clachnacuddin (10 Championships), Inverness Caledonian (5), Inverness Thistle (3 including the first in 1894) and Citadel (1).
- The reason for the above statistic is that until the admission of Buckie Thistle in 1909/10, the Highland League was made exclusively of Invernesian teams.
- Aberdeen 'A' was the first club to break the Inverness monopoly of the Highland League, taking the title in 1913.

Highland League Championship Wins

18	Inverness Caledonian*& Clachnacuddin
14	Elgin City** (inc. 1 withheld)
8	Buckie Thistle & Inverness Thistle*
7	Huntly
6	Keith
5	Peterhead**
4	Fraserburgh
3	Ross County#
2	Aberdeen 'A' & Deveronvale
1	Citadel (Inverness), Rothes, Nairn County, Forres Mechanics & Cove, Rangers

*Inverness Caledonian and Inverness Thistle merged in 1994 to form Inverness Caledonian Thistle and resigned from the Highland League to join the Scottish League.
**Resigned from the Highland League in 1999/00 to join the Scottish League.
Resigned from the Highland League in 1993/94 with Inverness Caledonian and Thistle to join the Scottish League.

The Centenary Highland League Championship of 1993 was withheld after Elgin City finished the season four points clear as Champions. Elgin City had requested that the last match of the season – the title decider – be brought forward by 24 hours to accommodate a friendly with Dundee due to be played on the Sunday. The HFL agreed, Elgin won and took the flag. However, it was soon revealed that had Elgin's game gone ahead on the Saturday as planned, two of their players would have been ineligible through suspension. The League committee voted unanimously to strip them of the title, finding that, by not informing them of the suspensions, City had brought the game into disrepute.

- Deveronvale won the 100th Highland League Championship in 2005/06.
- Forres Mechanics go by the nickname of The Can Cans.
- To the uninitiated, the name Inverurie Locos seems to be inspired by an urge to emulate the wild and exciting monikers of the USA's now defunct NASL. However, the team's full name – Inverurie Loco Works – reveals the club's origin as a works XI.
- Fraserburgh FC's black and white striped shirts have their origins in the 1890s and a local fishmonger with a Geordie connection. Subsequently, in the aftermath of the Second World War, when clothing was under ration and the Highland side found themselves without a strip, Newcastle United stepped in with a donation of used jerseys.
- Huntly FC had their Christie Park ground closed down in 1975 following an assault on referee George Macrae. In the ensuing enquiry, it was revealed that Huntly had failed to engage the services of the police at the match. The club was fined £100.

- In 1948, Highland League club Keith had to seek special permission from the Ministry of Labour and the Department of Agriculture to field former German POW Frank Hucker.

≈≈≈

Teams to have won both top and second tier Championships

Dumbarton
(Champions 1890/91*, 1891/92, Division 2**1910/11, 1971/72)

Dundee
(Champions 1962/63, Division 2**1946/47, Division 1# 1978/79 1991/92 1997/98)

Dundee Utd
(Champions 1982/83, Division 2**1924/25, 1928/29)

Hearts
(Champions 1894/95, 1896/97, 1957/58, 1959/60, Division 1# 1979/80)

Hibernian
(Champions 1902/03, 1947/48, 1950/51, 1951/52, Division 1# 1980/81, 1998/99, Division 2**1893/94, 1894/95, 1932/33)

Kilmarnock
(Champions 1964/65, Division 2**1897/98, 1898/99)

Motherwell
(Champions 1931/32, Division 1# 1981/82, 1984/85, Division 2**1953/54, 1968/69)

*Championship held jointly with Rangers.
**The old Division 2, second tier from 1893/94 – 1974/75.
The new Division 1, second tier from 1975/76 – present day.

- Greenock Morton have been champions of the old Second (1949/50, 1963/64, 1966/67), the new First (1977/78, 1983/84, 1986/87), the new Second (1998/99) and the new Third (1995/96) Divisions.
- Livingston have been promoted through every existing division as champions: Third Division 1995/96, Second Division 1998/99, First Division 2000/01.

≋

They are the Champions, my Friend

11 clubs have been Scottish champions. They are….

Rangers	51 titles
Celtic	40
Aberdeen	4
Hearts	4
Hibernian	4
Dumbarton	2
Third Lanark	1
Motherwell	1
Dundee	1
Kilmarnock	1
Dundee Utd	1

≋

34 teams have been second tier champions. They are…

Falkirk (7 titles); Ayr United, Greenock Morton, Raith Rovers, St Johnstone (all 6); Clyde, Hibernian, Partick Thistle (all 5); Dundee, Motherwell, St Mirren, Stirling Albion (all 4); Airdrieonians, Cowdenbeath, Dunfermline Athletic, Hamilton Academical, Leith

Athletic, (all 3); Kilmarnock, St Bernard's, Abercorn, Dundee Utd, Third Lanark, Queen's Park, Dumbarton (all 2); Port Glasgow Athletic, Alloa Athletic, Bo'ness, East Stirlingshire, Albion Rovers, East Fife, Queen of The South, Hearts, Livingston, Inverness Caledonian Thistle (all 1 title).

~~~

22 teams have won the third tier championship. They are…

Clyde, Brechin City, Stirling Albion (all 3 titles); Ayr United, Stranraer (both 2); Berwick Rangers, Clydebank, Falkirk, Queen's Park, Forfar Athletic, Montrose, Gretna, Dunfermline Ath, Meadowbank Thistle, Albion Rovers, Queen of the South, Dumbarton, Greenock Morton, Livingston, Partick Thistle, Raith Rovers, Airdrie United (all 1 title).

~~~

12 different clubs have won the fourth tier championship, each winning it once. They are….

Cowdenbeath, Gretna, Stranraer, Greenock Morton, Brechin City, Hamilton Academicals, Queen's Park, Ross County, Alloa Athletic, Inverness Caledonian Thistle, Livingston, Forfar Athletic.

The first ever Scottish League competition in 1890/91 –

with no relegation and no goal difference/average to split teams tied on points – finished thus:

	P	W	D	L	F	A	Pts.
Dumbarton	18	13	3	2	61	21	29
Rangers	18	13	3	2	58	25	29
Celtic	18	11	3	4	48	21	21
Cambuslang	18	8	4	6	47	42	20
Third Lanark	18	8	3	7	38	39	15
Hearts	18	6	2	10	31	37	14
Abercorn	18	5	2	11	36	47	12
St Mirren	18	5	1	12	39	62	11
Vale of Leven	18	5	1	12	27	65	11
Cowlairs	18	3	4	11	24	50	6

Gaffers

"Although we are playing Russian Roulette we are obviously playing Catch 22 at the moment and it's a difficult scenario to get my head round.".
Paul Sturrock

Managers to Have Led a Club to a Major Scottish Trophy Never Having Played Football in the Scottish League

Dick Advocaat
Wim Jansen*
Martin O'Neill

*Jansen, a former Dutch international, was the first non-Scot to win the Scottish League.

- Dundee Utd's Ivan Golac was the first non-Scot to lift a Scottish trophy as a manager. The ex-Yugoslavia international won the Scottish Cup in 1994.

- Only one manager has won the Scottish League Cup with two different clubs: Scot Symon, with East Fife in 1949/50 and with Rangers in 1960/61, 1961/62, 1963/64 and 1964/65.

- No manager has led two different clubs to the League Flag in Scotland. A Scottish manager, however, is one of only three bosses to have taken two different clubs to the English title: Kenny Dalglish with Liverpool and Blackburn*.

*The English managers in question were Herbert Chapman (Huddersfield Town and Arsenal) and Brian Clough (Derby County and Nottingham Forest).

~~~

Willie Maley served as Celtic manager for 43 years.

Championship-Winning Managers of the Modern Era

Season	Champions	Manager
1965/66	Celtic	Jock Stein
1966/67	Celtic	Jock Stein
1967/68	Celtic	Jock Stein
1968/69	Celtic	Jock Stein
1969/70	Celtic	Jock Stein
1970/71	Celtic	Jock Stein
1971/72	Celtic	Jock Stein
1972/73	Celtic	Jock Stein
1973/74	Celtic	Jock Stein
1974/75	Rangers	Jock Wallace
1975/76	Rangers	Jock Wallace
1976/77	Celtic	Jock Stein
1977/78	Rangers	Jock Wallace
1978/79	Celtic	Billy McNeill
1979/80	Aberdeen	Alex Ferguson
1980/81	Celtic	Billy McNeill
1981/82	Celtic	Billy McNeill
1982/83	Dundee Utd	Jim McLean
1983/84	Aberdeen	Alex Ferguson
1984/85	Aberdeen	Alex Ferguson
1985/86	Celtic	Davie Hay
1986/87	Rangers	Graeme Souness
1987/88	Celtic	Billy McNeill
1988/89	Rangers	Graeme Souness
1989/90	Rangers	Graeme Souness
1990/91	Rangers	Souness/Walter Smith
1991/92	Rangers	Walter Smith
1992/93	Rangers	Walter Smith
1993/94	Rangers	Walter Smith
1994/95	Rangers	Walter Smith
1995/96	Rangers	Walter Smith

1996/97	Rangers	Walter Smith
1997/98	Celtic	Wim Jansen*
1998/99	Rangers	Dick Advocaat
1999/00	Rangers	Dick Advocaat
2000/01	Celtic	Martin O'Neill
2001/02	Celtic	Martin O'Neill
2002/03	Rangers	Alex McLeish
2003/04	Celtic	Martin O'Neill
2004/05	Rangers	Alex McLeish
2005/06	Celtic	Gordon Strachan

≈≈≈

Scottish Championship Manager Leaderboard

William Struth (Rangers)	18
Willie Maley (Celtic)	16
Jock Stein (Celtic)	10
William Wilton (Rangers)	10
Walter Smith (Rangers)	7
Scot Symon (Rangers)	6
Graeme Souness (Rangers)	4
Hugh Shaw (Hibernian)	3
Jock Wallace (Rangers)	3
Billy McNeill (Celtic)	3
Alex Ferguson (Aberdeen)	3
Martin O'Neill (Celtic)	3
Tommy Walker (Hearts)	2
Dick Advocaat (Rangers)	2
Alex McLeish (Rangers)	2
Edward Tarbat (Third Lanark)	1
John "Sailor" Hunter (Motherwell)	1
Jimmy McGrory (Celtic)	1
David Halliday (Aberdeen)	1

Bob Shankly (Dundee)	1
Willie Waddell (Kilmarnock)	1
Jim McLean (Dundee Utd)	1
Davie Hay (Celtic)	1
Wim Jansen (Celtic)	1
Gordon Strachan (Celtic)	1

≈≈≈

Scottish managers to have won the English Championship in the Post-War Era

Alex Ferguson (Manchester United)*
George Graham (Arsenal)
Kenny Dalglish (Liverpool & Blackburn)
Dave Mackay (Derby County)
Bill Shankly (Liverpool)
Matt Busby (Manchester United)

*Sir Alex Ferguson is the only manager to have led sides to both the Scottish and English Championships

≈≈≈

Scottish Cup-Winning Managers of the Modern Era

1960	Rangers	Scot Symon
1961	Dunfermline	Jock Stein
1962	Rangers	Scot Symon
1963	Rangers	Scot Symon
1964	Rangers	Scot Symon
1965	Celtic	Jock Stein
1966	Rangers	Scot Symon
1967	Celtic	Jock Stein
1968	Dunfermline	George Farm
1969	Celtic	Jock Stein
1970	Aberdeen	Eddie Turnbull
1971	Celtic	Jock Stein

1972	Celtic	Jock Stein
1973	Rangers	Jock Wallace
1974	Celtic	Jock Stein
1975	Celtic	Jock Stein
1976	Rangers	Jock Wallace
1977	Celtic	Jock Stein
1978	Rangers	Jock Wallace
1979	Rangers	John Greig
1980	Celtic	Billy McNeill
1981	Rangers	John Greig
1982	Aberdeen	Alex Ferguson
1983	Aberdeen	Alex Ferguson
1984	Aberdeen	Alex Ferguson
1985	Celtic	Davie Hay
1986	Aberdeen	Alex Ferguson
1987	St Mirren	Alex Smith
1988	Celtic	Billy McNeill
1989	Celtic	Billy McNeill
1990	Aberdeen	Alex Smith & Jocky Scott
1991	Motherwell	Tommy McLean
1992	Rangers	Walter Smith
1993	Rangers	Walter Smith
1994	Dundee Utd	Ivan Golac
1995	Celtic	Tommy Burns
1996	Rangers	Walter Smith
1997	Kilmarnock	Bobby Williamson
1998	Hearts	Jim Jeffries
1999	Rangers	Dick Advocaat
2000	Rangers	Dick Advocaat
2001	Celtic	Martin O'Neill
2002	Rangers	Alex McLeish
2003	Rangers	Alex McLeish
2004	Celtic	Martin O'Neill
2005	Celtic	Martin O'Neill
2006	Hearts	Valdas Ivanauskas

Scottish League Cup Winning Managers

1946-47	Rangers	William Struth
1947-48	East Fife	Scot Symon
1948-49	Rangers	William Struth
1949-50	East Fife	Scot Symon
1950-51	Motherwell	George Stevenson
1951-52	Dundee	George Anderson
1952-53	Dundee	George Anderson
1953-54	East Fife	Scot Symon
1954-55	Hearts	Tommy Walker
1955-56	Aberdeen	Dave Shaw
1956-57	Celtic	Jimmy McGrory
1957-58	Celtic	Jimmy McGrory
1958-59	Hearts	Tommy Walker
1959-60	Hearts	Tommy Walker
1960-61	Rangers	Scot Symon
1961-62	Rangers	Scot Symon
1962-63	Hearts	Tommy Walker
1963-64	Rangers	Scot Symon
1964-65	Rangers	Scot Symon
1965-66	Celtic	Jock Stein
1966-67	Celtic	Jock Stein
1967-68	Celtic	Jock Stein
1968-69	Celtic	Jock Stein
1969-70	Celtic	Jock Stein
1970-71	Rangers	Willie Waddell
1971-72	Partick Thistle	Davie McParland
1972-73	Hibernian	Eddie Turnbull
1973-74	Dundee	Davie White
1974-75	Celtic	Jock Stein
1975-76	Rangers	Jock Wallace
1976-77	Aberdeen	Ally MacLeod
1977-78	Rangers	Jock Wallace
1978-79	Rangers	John Greig

1979-80	Dundee Utd	Jim McLean
1980-81	Dundee Utd	Jim McLean
1981-82	Rangers	John Greig
1982-83	Celtic	Billy McNeill
1983-84	Rangers	Jock Wallace
1984-85	Rangers	Jock Wallace
1985-86	Aberdeen	Alex Ferguson
1986-87	Rangers	Graeme Souness
1987-88	Rangers	Graeme Souness
1988-89	Rangers	Graeme Souness
1989-90	Aberdeen	Jocky Scott & Alex Smith
1990-91	Rangers	Graeme Souness
1991-92	Hibernian	Alex Miller
1992-93	Rangers	Walter Smith
1993-94	Rangers	Walter Smith
1994-95	Raith Rovers	Jimmy Nicol
1995-96	Aberdeen	Roy Aitken
1996-97	Rangers	Walter Smith
1997-98	Celtic	Wim Jansen
1998-99	Rangers	Dick Advocaat
1999-00	Celtic	Kenny Dalglish
2000-01	Celtic	Martin O'Neill
2001-02	Rangers	Alex McLeish
2002-03	Rangers	Alex McLeish
2003/04	Livingston	Davie Hay
2004/05	Rangers	Alex Mcleish
2005/06	Celtic	Gordon Strachan

Championship Winning Managers Who Have Also Won the Scottish League as a Player

Willie Maley – Celtic (Manager & Player)
Jimmy McGrory – Celtic (Manager & Player)
Scot Symon – Rangers (Manager & Player)
Davie Hay – Celtic (Manager & Player)
Billy McNeill – Celtic (Manager & Player)
Graeme Souness – Rangers (Manager & Player)*
Alex McLeish – Rangers (Manager) Aberdeen
(Player)
Gordon Strachan – Celtic (Manager) Aberdeen
(Player)
*Unlike the others, Souness was simultaneously player
and manager.

≈≈≈

Matt Busby is the only football figure to be mentioned
anywhere in a Beatles lyric – his name features in a
litany along with BB King and Doris Day in the *Let it
Be* track *Dig It*.

≈≈≈

Scottish Cup Winning Managers Who Have Also Won the Scottish Cup as a Player

Willie Maley – Celtic (Manager & Player)
Jock Stein – Celtic (Manager & Player)
John Greig – Rangers (Manager & Player)
Davie Hay – Celtic (Manager & Player)
Billy McNeill – Celtic (Manager & Player)
Tommy McLean – Motherwell (Manager)
& Rangers (Player)
Tommy Burns – Celtic (Manager & Player)
Alex McLeish – Rangers (Manager) Aberdeen
(Player).

Note: Motherwell's Championship-winning manager of 1932, John "Sailor" Watson was still with the Steelmen in 1952 when they won the Scottish Cup, but had relinquished the manager's post six years earlier, holding the post of secretary at the time of the Cup win. As a player for Dundee he had won the Scottish Cup in 1910.

≈≈≈

Scottish League Cup Winning Managers Who Have Also Won the Scottish League Cup as a Player

John Greig – Rangers (Manager & Player)
Graeme Souness – Rangers (Manager & Player)*
Jocky Scott – Aberdeen (Co-manager& Player)**
Billy McNeill – Celtic (Manager & Player)
Alex Miller – Hibernian (Manager) & Rangers (Player)
Roy Aitken – Aberdeen (Manager) & Celtic (Player)
Kenny Dalglish – Celtic (Manager & Player)
Davie Hay – Livingston (Manager) & Celtic (Player)
Alex McLeish – Rangers (Manager) & Aberdeen (Player)

*Player-manager.
**Co-manager with Alex Smith.

Dunfermline manager George Farm, who led The Pars to victory in the 1968 Scottish Cup final over Hearts, had played in goal for Blackpool when they won the 1953 FA Cup Final – the game now known as the Matthews Final.

Rangers manager William Struth presided over the club's first League and Cup Double in 1928. He was still at Ibrox as manager when the club won their first Treble in 1949.

≈≈≈

John Hunter broke the longest period to date of Old Firm Championship domination – 27 years – by winning the League with Motherwell in 1931/32.

≈≈≈

For Rent: Flat in Gorgie Three Month Lease

Hearts hold an impressive record for managerial changes in the modern era. Since the appointment of John Harvey in 1966, upon the sacking of the legendary Tommy Walker, the family photos on the gaffer's desk have been changed 20 times:

Valdas Ivanauskas 22/3/2006 – Time of Writing*
Graham Rix 8/11/2005 – 22/3/2006 – Sacked
John McGlynn 21/10/2005 – 8/11/2005*
George Burley 30/6/2005 – 21/10/2005 – Sacked
John Robertson 3/11/2004 – 9/5/2005 – Sacked
Peter Houston 29/10/2004 – 1/11/2004**
Craig Levein 1/12/2000 – 29/10/2004*– Resigned
Peter Houston 8/11/2000 – 1/12/2000*
Jim Jeffries 1/8/1995 – 08/11/2000 – Resigned
Tommy McLean 1/7/1994 – 31/5/1995 – Sacked
Sandy Clark 10/5/1993 – 20/6/1994 – Sacked
Joe Jordan 10/9/1990 – 3/5/1993 – Sacked

Sandy Jardine 1/11/1986 – 30/11/1988 ¶
Alex MacDonald 1/1/1982 – 10/9/1990 – Sacked
Tony Ford 1/7/1981 – 31/12/1981 – Sacked
Bobby Moncur 1/8/1980 – 31/5/1981 – Resigned
Willie Ormond 1/08/1977 – 31/5/1980 – Sacked
John Hagart 1/8/1974 – 31/51977 – Sacked
Bobby Seith 1/7/1970 – 31/5/1974 – Sacked
John Harvey 1/8/1966 – 31/5/1970 – Resigned
*Caretaker,**Second stint as caretaker.
¶ Co-manager.

≈≈≈

Tommy Docherty's Managerial Career

Tommy Docherty once quipped he had "had more clubs than Jack Nicklaus". After a playing career with just three clubs – Celtic, Preston North End and Arsenal – he took to the dugout and helmed the following sides:

Chelsea 1961– 1967
Rotherham United 1967 – 1968
Queens Park Rangers 1968
Aston Villa 1968 – 1970
FC Porto 1970 – 1971
Hull City 1971 – 1972
Scotland 1972
Manchester United 1972 – 1977
Derby County 1977 – 1979
Queens Park Rangers 1979 – 1980
Sydney Olympic 1981
Preston North End 1981 – 1982
South Melbourne 1982 – 1983
Sydney Olympic 1983
Wolverhampton Wanderers 1984 – 1985
Altrincham 1987 – 1988

A quick word...

"John ... you're immortal".
Bill Shankly to Jock Stein in the immediate aftermath of Celtic's European Cup triumph of 1967.

"I don't believe everything Bill tells me about his players. Had they been that good, they'd not only have won the European Cup but the Ryder Cup, the Boat Race and even the Grand National".
Jock Stein on Bill Shankly before Celtic met Liverpool in the 1966 European Cup Winners' Cup.

"At one point, I thought it would end up 20-20. But common sense took over – boring football".
Alex Ferguson on his United side's 3-2 win at Craven Cottage in 2005.

"I am particularly sorry that it was John of all people who was involved – from what I know of him, he is an honest, hardworking lad who was only trying to do his job – as I was trying to do mine".
Jim McLean's apology – in his resignation statement – after assaulting BBC reporter John Barnes

- Rangers manager Scot Symon was sacked in November 1967 with his side unbeaten and sitting at the top of the league.
- Graeme Souness was sent off in his first match as player-manager of Rangers, at Easter Road against Hibs in 1986.
- Jock Wallace, then a Rangers coach, neglected to shake Celtic manager Jock Stein's hand after Rangers won the 1970 League Cup Final – a sin of omission for which his mother, who witnessed the heat-of-the-moment snub on television, gave her son such a telling off that he never again forgot to console a losing opponent.

- The architect of Hibernian's famous triple Championship winning side of the 40s and 50s did not live to see the fruits of his labours. Manager Willie McCartney died of a heart attack during a game in January 1948. His charges went on to win their first flag since 1903 in May 1948.
- Only two managers have won the Scottish Cup with two different clubs; Jock Stein with Dunfermline and Celtic and Alex Smith with St Mirren and Aberdeen.
- The only manager to lead a second tier side to victory in the Scottish Cup was Davie Mclean of East Fife in 1938.
- Before taking on the Lisbon Lions in the first round of the Scottish Cup at Celtic Park in January 1968, Dunfermline manager George Farm jokingly suggested that tickets should be printed in anticipation of a replay at East End Park. They were not needed. Dunfermline won 2-0 and went on to lift the trophy.
- St Johnstone have supplied the Scottish national team with two managers: Bobby Brown left Muirton Park for international duty in 1967 and was later followed by Willie Ormond, his successor at Perth, in 1973.
- Andy Roxburgh is the only Scotland manager to follow up qualification for a World Cup with qualification for a European Championship – the World Cup 1990 in Italy followed by the European Championships 1992 in Sweden.
- Scotland managers Jock Stein (with Celtic in 1954), Craig Brown (with Dundee in 1962), Ian McColl (six times with Rangers), Willie Ormond (three times with Hibernian) and Bobby Brown (three times with Rangers) all played with Scottish League Championship-winning sides.

Trust me – I Know What I'm talking About

Scotland managers to have been capped by Scotland as players:

Tommy Docherty – Preston North End & Arsenal – 25 caps
Ian McColl – Rangers – 14 caps
Andy Beattie – Preston North End – 7 caps
Willie Ormond – Hibernian – 6 caps
Bobby Brown – Rangers – 3 caps
Matt Busby – Manchester City – 1 cap
(The clubs stated are the clubs with which the player plied his trade when capped).

The World Cup

"What's wrong with a wee bit of optimism?"
Ally MacLeod

1930 – 1950

- Scotland – along with England – had withdrawn from FIFA in the 1920s and, as such, was ineligible to compete in the World Cups of 1930, 1934 and 1938.

- For the first World Cup after WWII, staged in Brazil in 1950, FIFA offered places at the finals to the top two in the Home International table for that year. Scotland came second, beating Wales 2-0 at Hampden, battering Northern Ireland 8-2 at Windsor Park, but going down by a single goal to nil at Hampden to England. But instead of packing the woolly jerseys for a stint in the Brazilian sunshine, the SFA snubbed the offer in a fit of cock-eyed nobility, insisting that if they could not qualify as British Champions then they were unworthy of the place. It is said that England captain Billy Wright pleaded with Scotland captain George Young to make the SFA see sense, but his appeals fell on deaf ears.

- It was left to Edward John McIlvenny (1924 – 1989), a Scot born in Greenock who had emigrated to the United States in 1949 – to leave the first significant tartan fingerprint on World Cup history. McIlvenny was made captain-for-the-day against England, with Walter Bahr stepping aside because McIlvenny "was British". The USA won 1-0.

1954 – Switzerland

- Rangers refused to release any of their players as they had already committed them to a summer tour of the United States.
- Aberdeen's Fred Martin was custodian for the 7-0 defeat to Uruguay. He had been signed by Aberdeen as an inside-right, but was later converted to goalkeeper.
- Fred Martin's next two internationals were against the Hungary of Ferenc Puskas (a 4-2 loss at Hampden) and a 7-2 horsing from England at Wembley, bringing his goals conceded tally in three consecutive internationals to 18.
- Hibernian's Willie Ormond started both games of the 1954 campaign. Twenty years later he became the only man to both play for and manage Scotland at the World Cup Finals.
- Scotland's heaviest World Cup defeat came at the hands of Uruguay to the tune of 7-0.
- Scotland's 1954 World Cup squad comprised only 13 players.

Pool Three

	P	W	D	L	F	A	Pts
Uruguay	2	2	0	0	9	0	4
Austria	2	2	0	0	6	0	4
Czechoslovakia	2	0	0	2	0	7	0
Scotland	2	0	0	2	0	8	0

Austria 1 Scotland 0

Sportzplatz Hardturm, Zurich 16 June.

Austria: Probst (32 mins).

Uruguay 7 Scotland 0

St Jakob Stadium, Basle 19 June.

Uruguay: Borges (17, 48 & 58 mins), Miguez (31 mins), Abbadie (55 & 84 mins), (82 mins).

1958 – Sweden

- Scotland qualified at the expense of Spain and Switzerland.
- Hearts' Jimmy Murray earned Scotland a draw with Yugoslavia in their first match of the tournament – Scotland's first ever World Cup goal and point.
- Tommy Docherty travelled with the squad but did not compete on the field.
- The legendary Just Fontaine scored France's second goal against Scotland, his eventual goal tally reaching 13 for the tournament. His high scoring record still stands.
- Manchester United's Matt Busby would have been Scotland manager in Sweden, but for his ongoing recovery in the wake of the Munich air tragedy. In the event, the squad was selected by committee, with trainer Dawson Walker taking charge of team affairs.

Pool Two

	P	W	D	L	F	A	Pts
France	3	2	0	1	11	7	4
Yugoslavia	3	1	2	0	7	6	4
Paraguay	3	1	1	1	9	12	3
Scotland	3	0	1	2	4	6	1

Yugoslavia 1 Scotland 1
Arosvallen, Västerås 8 June.
Yugoslavia: Petacovic (13 mins); Scotland: Jimmy Murray (48 mins).

Paraguay 3 Scotland 2
Idrottsparken, Norrköping 11 June.
Paraguay: Aguero (4 mins), Re (44 mins), Parodi (74 mins); Scotland: Jackie Mudie (23 mins), Bobby Collins (76 mins).

France 2 Scotland 1
Eyravallen, Örebo 15 June.
France: Kopa (22 mins), Fontaine (45 mins);
Scotland: Sammy Baird (66 mins).

1974 – West Germany

- To qualify, Scotland knocked out European Champions-in-waiting Czechoslovakia.
- The World Cup Squad made its debut on the singles chart with Scotland's first official World Cup song, *Easy Easy*, which peaked at number 20. The album – *Scotland, Scotland* (Polydor 2383282) – is valued in the *Record Collector Rare Record Price Guide 2006* at £12 in mint condition.
- Peter Lorimer ended a Scottish World Cup goal drought of 16 years and one day when he opened the scoring against Zaïre.
- Denis Law played his one-and-only World Cup game against Zaïre in the opening match. It was his 50th and last Scotland cap.
- Scotland returned home from West Germany unbeaten, and remained the only undefeated side in the tournament – the hosts and eventual winners had been defeated at the group stage by East Germany.
- Hibernian's Eric Schaedler, the son of a German POW, made Willie Ormond's 22 but did not start a match.
- Celtic's Danny McGrain played in all three of Scotland's matches and established his reputation as a world-class full-back despite suffering from dehydration throughout the tournament. When he returned to Scotland, he was diagnosed as diabetic. He went on to win 62 caps.
- A favourite chant of the Tartan Army of the day

celebrated Scotland's Manchester United centre half. It went: "Six foot two, eyes of blue, Big Jim Holton's after you." Pedants should note that Jim Holton was six foot one.

- Scotland recorded a first ever World Cup win in this its third tournament.
- Joe Jordan and David Hay became the first Scots to be booked at the World Cup in the final game against Yugoslavia.
- Willie Ormond's squad comprised 12 Anglos and ten home-based players.
- Celtic's Kenny Dalglish made his World Cup debut in 1974.
- The unbeaten squad came home to a rapturous reception.

Group 2

	P	W	D	L	F	A	Pts
Yugoslavia	3	1	2	0	10	1	4
Brazil	3	1	2	0	3	0	4
Scotland	3	1	2	0	3	1	4
Zaïre	3	0	0	3	0	14	0

Scotland 2 Zaïre 0
Wesfalenstadion, Dortmund 14 June.
Scotland: Peter Lorimer (26 mins), Joe Jordan (34 mins).

Scotland 0 Brazil 0
Waldstadion, Frankfurt 18 June.

Yugoslavia 1 Scotland 1
Waldstadion, Frankfurt 22 June.
Yugoslavia: Karasi (81 mins); Scotland: Joe Jordan (88 mins).

1978 – Argentina

- To qualify, Scotland had seen off both European Champions Czechoslovakia and Wales.
- The official World Cup song (featuring the squad with Rod Stewart) was *Ole Ola (Muhler Brasileira)*, which peaked at number four in late May 1978. Rangers-supporting Glaswegian comedian and Bobby Darin fan Andy Cameron weighed in with *Ally's Tartan Army*. It reached number 6 in the chart, peaking in the week of – when else? – the 1st of April, a full two months before the World Cup kicked off.
- A paying crowd gave the Scots an Argentina send-off party from Hampden. 25,000 souls attended the event, which was also televised live.
- Andranik Eskandarian – who put through his own posts for Scotland's only goal against Iran – landed a lucrative deal with the New York Cosmos after the World Cup. His son went on the play for DC United in MLS.
- The Scots' kit was manufactured by Umbro and featured flared tracksuit bottoms.
- Three of the 22 squad players sported perms for the finals: Alan Rough, Asa Hartford and Derek Johnstone※.
- MacLeod before the finals: "I think we'll bring back a medal; I just hope it's gold".
- Ally MacLeod during the finals, at a press conference after the 1-1 draw with Iran, as a mongrel dog sidled up to him: "Look – my only friend"#.
- Ally MacLeod after the finals: "Looking back on Argentina now, people remember they enjoyed themselves. At all the other World Cups we didn't have the same fun. And the end result was just the same…".
- Squad member Sandy Jardine: "All we ever hear

is that Argentina was Ally's fault. He was partly to blame, so were his coaches, 22 players and the SFA."

- Willie Johnston was banned for life for when traces of the banned substance Fencamfanin showed up in his urine test.
- Ally MacLeod's squad was made up of 15 Anglos and 7 home-based Scots.
* Graeme Souness maintains that his hair was naturally curly.
# In the popular – but untrue – punchline to this tale, the dog proceeds to bite the hapless manager as he pats it.

Group 4

	P	W	D	L	F	A	Pts
Peru	3	2	1	0	7	2	5
Holland	3	1	1	1	5	3	3
Scotland	3	1	1	1	5	6	3
Iran	3	0	1	2	2	8	1

Peru 3 Scotland 1
Estadio Chateau Carreras, Córdoba 3 June.
Peru: Cueto (43 mins), Cubillas (72 & 77 mins);
Scotland: Joe Jordan (14 mins).

Scotland 1 Iran 1
Estadio Chateau Carreras, Córdoba 7 June.
Scotland: Eskandarian (43 mins, og);
Iran: Daniaeifard (60 mins).

Holland 2 Scotland 3
Estadio Cuidad de Mendoza, Mendoza 11 June.
Holland: Rensenbrink (34 mins, pen), Rep (71 mins); Scotland: Kenny Dalglish (44 mins), Archie Gemmill (47 mins pen & 68 mins).

NB: The Scots went into the match against Holland needing to win by three clear goals to qualify for the second phase. They led by 3-1 until the 71st minute.

1982 – Spain

- To qualify, Scotland topped their group of Northern Ireland, Sweden, Portugal and Israel.
- The World Cup song was *We Have A Dream*, featuring the squad and *Gregory's Girl* star John Gordon Sinclair. Written by BA Robertson, it reached number 5 on the chart.
- Joe Jordan scored at his third consecutive World Cup.
- Scotland eliminated on goal difference for the third successive finals.
- Kenny Dalglish and Joe Jordan played at their third and final World Cup.
- Joe Jordan became the first player to belong to a non-British club side (AC Milan) to represent Scotland at the finals.
- John Wark was Scotland's top scorer with two goals.
- Scotland's manager Jock Stein, in marked contrast to his ebullient predecessor, Ally MacLeod: "I do not think that it is imaginable that we would ever win the World Cup. That is dreaming.".
- Stein on Scotland's weakest spot: "Our fear is not our opponents. Our fear is ourselves".
- Tartan Army banner at the New Zealand match: "Don't Worry Lads, Ally MacLeod is in Blackpool".
- World Cup debutantes New Zealand pegged the Scots' 3-0 lead back to 3-2 before two late goals restored the three goal margin.
- Jock Stein's squad was made up of 11 Anglos, one player from Serie A and nine home-based Scots.

Group 6

	P	W	D	L	F	A	Pts
Brazil	3	3	0	0	10	2	6
Soviet Union	3	1	1	1	6	4	3
Scotland	3	1	1	1	8	8	3
New Zealand	3	0	0	3	2	12	0

Scotland 5 New Zealand 2
Estadio la Rosaleda, Malaga 15 June.
Scotland: Kenny Dalglish (18 mins), John Wark
(29 and 32 mins), John Robertson (73 mins), Steve
Archibald (79 mins); New Zealand: Sumner (54 mins),
Wooddin (64 mins).

Brazil 4 Scotland 1
Estadio Benito Villamarin, Seville 18 June.
Brazil: Zico (33 mins), Bernardi (48 mins), Élder
(63 mins), Falcâo (87 mins); Scotland: David Narey
(18 mins).

USSR 2 Scotland 2
Estadio la Rosaleda, Malaga 22 June.
USSR: Chivadze (59 mins), Shengelia (84 mins);
Scotland: Joe Jordan (15 mins), Graeme Souness
(86 mins).

1986 – Mexico

- Scotland had come second to Spain in qualification, and won through to Mexico via a play-off with Australia.
- No World Cup song charted.
- Aberdeen's Alex Ferguson took Scotland to the finals following the death of Jock Stein during Scotland's final group qualifying match at Ninian Park, Cardiff.
- Gordon Strachan scored the Scots' only goal in the "Group of Death".

- Kenny Dalglish was selected for his fourth consecutive World Cup Finals, but had to withdraw through injury.
- Alex Ferguson's squad was made up of seven Anglos, one player each from La Liga (Spain) and Serie A and 13 home-based Scots.

Group E

	P	W	D	L	F	A	Pts
Denmark	3	3	0	0	9	1	6
West Germany	3	1	1	1	3	4	3
Uruguay	3	0	2	1	2	7	2
Scotland	3	0	1	2	1	3	1

Denmark 1 Scotland 0
Estadio Neza, Nezahualcóyotl, 4 June .
Denmark: Elkjær-Larsen (58 mins).
West Germany 2 Scotland 1
Estadio La Corregidora, Santiago de Querétaro
8 June.
W. Germany: Völler (22 mins), Allofs (50 mins);
Scotland: Gordon Strachan (18 mins).
Scotland 0 Uruguay 0
Estadio Neza, Nezahualcóyotl, 13 June.

1990 – Italy

- Scotland qualified behind Yugoslavia and at the expense of France, Norway and Cyprus.
- The official World Cup single hit its nadir with the lowest ever chart position of 45 for *Say it With Pride*.
- The defeat of Sweden was Scotland's first World Cup victory in eight years.
- "I don't think you can really print how I felt by the end of it all." Italia '90 veteran Maurice Malpas still wasn't over the 1-0 reverse at the hands of Costa

Rica some 12 years after the game, writing in the *Scotland on Sunday*.

- Andy Roxburgh's squad was made up of eight Anglos, two players from the German Bundesliga and 12 home-based players.

Group C

	P	W	D	L	F	A	Pts
Brazil	3	3	0	0	4	1	6
Costa Rica	3	2	0	1	3	2	4
Scotland	3	1	0	2	2	3	2
Sweden	3	0	0	3	3	6	0

Costa Rica 1 Scotland 0

Stadio Luigi Ferraris, Genoa 11 June.

Cayasso (49 mins).

Scotland 2 Sweden 1

Stadio Luigi Ferraris, Genoa 16 June.

Scotland: Stuart McCall (10 mins), Maurice Johnston (80 mins, pen); Sweden: Strömberg (86 mins).

Brazil 1 Scotland 0

Stadio delle Alpi 20 June.

Brazil: Müller (82 mins).

1998 – France

- Scotland qualified with Austria, knocking out Sweden, Latvia, Estonia and Belarus.
- Scotland's World Cup song was written and performed by Del Amitri. *Don't Come Home Too Soon*, a wistful ballad informed by the experiences of 20 years since Argentina, made number 15 in the charts.
- On 9 October 1996, Scotland kicked-off in Talinn, only for the referee to abandon the match as soon as Billy Dodds touched the ball to John Collins. Estonia had failed to show as a result of a dispute over floodlights.

- "Scotland were afraid of us. They had injuries and they had suspensions and we think that they wanted to avoid this match." Estonian FA president Laver Pohlak on why he thought Scotland had complained about the Estonian floodlights.
- Scotland took on World Champions Brazil in the showpiece opening match.
- Tom Boyd scored Scotland's first World Cup own goal, giving Brazil a 2-1 win.
- On the day of the match, the *Daily Record* reported a saltire-shaped cloud formation in the Paris sky at dusk, claiming it as an historic good omen.
- Between the 1-1 draw with Norway and the 3-0 defeat at the hands of Morocco, Craig Burley peroxided his hair. Burley and his new 'do were both given their marching orders in the final match – the first Scot to be sent off in a World Cup.

Group A

	P	W	D	L	F	A	Pts
Brazil	3	2	0	1	6	3	6
Norway	3	1	2	0	5	4	5
Morocco	3	1	1	1	5	5	4
Scotland	3	0	1	2	2	6	1

Brazil 2 Scotland 1

Stade de France, Paris 10 June.

Brazil: César Sampaio (4), Tom Boyd (73 mins og);

Scotland: John Collins (38 pen).

Scotland 1 Norway 1

Parc Lescure, Bordeaux 16 June.

Scotland: Craig Burley (66 mins);

Norway: H Flo (46 mins).

Scotland 0 Morocco 3

Stade Geoffroy-Guichard, St Étienne 23 June.

Morocco: Bassir (22 mins, 85 mins), Hadda (46 mins).

Goal!

Scotland's goal tally at World Cups stands at 24*. They were scored by:

4	Joe Jordan	(Leeds Utd, Manchester Utd & AC Milan)
2	John Wark	(Ipswich Town)
	Kenny Dalglish	(Liverpool)
	Archie Gemmill	(Nottingham Forest)
1	Jimmy Murray	(Hearts)
	Jackie Mudie	(Blackpool)
	Bobby Collins	(Celtic)
	Sammy Baird	(Rangers)
	Peter Lorimer	(Leeds Utd)
	John Robertson	(Nottingham Forest)
	Steve Archibald	(Tottenham Hotspur)
	David Narey	(Dundee Utd)
	Graeme Souness	(Liverpool)
	Gordon Strachan	(Manchester Utd)
	Stuart McCall	(Everton)
	Maurice Johnston	(Rangers)
	John Collins	(Monaco)
	Craig Burley	(Celtic)

*The Scots were also beneficiaries of an own goal, courtesy of Andranik Eskandarian.

Scotland's World Cup Managers

Andy Beattie 1954*
Dawson Walker 1958**
Willie Ormond 1974
Ally MacLeod 1978
Jock Stein 1982
Alex Ferguson 1986#
Andy Roxburgh 1990
Craig Brown 1998

*Simultaneously manager of Huddersfield Town.
**Trainer who deputised for Matt Busby following Munich air tragedy.
Simultaneously Aberdeen manager.

Scotland's World Cup Captains

Colin Hendry of Blackburn Rovers (v. Brazil, Norway and Morocco 1998)
Roy Aitken of Newcastle Utd (v. Costa Rica, Sweden and Brazil, 1990)
Willie Miller of Aberdeen (v. Uruguay 1986)
Graeme Souness of Sampdoria (v. USSR and Brazil 1982) and Rangers (v. Denmark and W Germany 1986)
Danny McGrain of Celtic (v. New Zealand 1982)
Archie Gemmill of Nottingham Forest (v. Iran 1978)
Bruce Rioch of Derby Country (v. Peru and Holland 1978)
Billy Bremner of Leeds Utd (v. Zaïre, Brazil and Yugoslavia 1974)
Bobby Evans of Celtic (v. France 1958)
Tommy Younger of Liverpool (v. Yugoslavia and Paraguay 1958)
Willie Cunningham of Preston North End (v. Austria and Uruguay 1954)

The Worst (and Best) World Cup Football Songs of All Time

In 2006, Littlewoods Pools conducted a poll of 1500 British football fans to find the top (and bottom) World Cup anthems. The results were as follows:

Worst

1 *This Time (We'll Get It Right)* England World Cup Squad, 1982*.
2 *(How Does It Feel To Be) On Top of the World* Spice Girls & Lightning Seeds, 1998.
3 *Hey Baby* World Cup remix DJ Otzi, 2002.
4 *Top of the World* Chumbawamba, 1998.
5 *We Have a Dream* Scotland World Cup Squad, 1982**.
6 *We're on the Ball* Ant and Dec, 2002.
7 *Over There* The Babe Team, 2002.
8 *We've Got the Whole World at Our Feet* England World Cup Squad, 1986.
9 *Easy Easy* Scotland World Cup Squad, 1974.
10 *Goldenballs (Mr Beckham to You)* Bell & Spurling, 2002.

Best

1 *World in Motion*, New Order and England Squad, 1990.
2 *Nessun Dorma*, Luciano Pavarotti, 1990.
3 *Three Lions* 98, The Lightning Seeds, featuring Baddiel & Skinner, remixed in 1998#.
4 *Vindaloo* Fat Les, 1998.
5 *World Cup Willie* Lonnie Donegan, 1966##.
6 *Jerusalem* Fat Les, 2000.
7 *Don't Come Home Too Soon* Del Amitri;¶
8 *Back Home* England World Cup Squad, 1970.
9 *The Great Escape* England supporters' band, 1998.

10 *Olé Ola* Rod Stewart and Scotland World Cup Squad, 1978.§

*B-side features *Fly the Flag*, the tune to the Tartan Army favourite *We Hate Jimmy Hill*.

**Features a spoken "vocal" from John Gordon Sinclair detailing a dream in which Nottingham Forest's John Robertson is handing the ball to our protagonist so that he may score the winning goal for Scotland in the World Cup final.

Features the dissenting voice of ex-Scotland international Alan Hansen bemoaning a poor England performance.

Only example of a Scot – Donegan was born in Glasgow – recording England's World Cup Song.

¶ Did not feature the squad as chorus.

§ Following the Peru and Iran results, Rod's Latin-flavoured party track dropped 9 places from number 4 to 13, the biggest faller in the top 20 in the week ending 17 June 1978.

As a footnote, following their Mercury Prize win of 2004, Franz Ferdinand lead singer Alex Kapranos offered his band's services as official Scotland balladeers for Germany 2006. Unfortunately, their services were not required.

Scotland Cannae Dae it cos they Didnae Qualify*

We know what you didn't do last summer: tales of woe from the non-qualification years.

*Paraphrase of Andy Cameron's line "England cannae dae it cos they didnae qualify" from his 1978 smash hit, *Ally's Tartan Army*.

1962 – Chile

Finishing even on points with Czechoslovakia in the qualifying group, the two sides faced each other in a play-off at the Heysel Stadium, Brussels in November 1961. After extra time, the Czechs ran out 4-2 winners, with Ian St John netting both of Scotland's strikes. Eddie Connachan (Dunfermline Athletic); Alex Hamilton (Dundee), Eric Caldow (Rangers); Pat Crerand (Celtic), Ian Ure (Dundee), Jim Baxter (Rangers); Ralph Brand (Rangers), John White (Tottenham Hotspur), Ian St John (Liverpool), Denis Law (Torino), Hugh Robertson (Dundee) made up the side.

- Tottenham Hotspur's John White from the above team, a Double winner with Spurs in 1961 and European Cup Winners' Cup winner in 1963 was killed at the age of 27 in 1964 when struck by lightning on a golf course.

1966 – England

Suffered an unexpected reverse at the hands of Poland at Hampden Park and following a famous 1-0 home win over Italy – in which John Greig scored – travelled to Naples for the decider, going down 3-0.

The Scotland side that lost to Italy (managed by Celtic's Jock Stein): Adam Blacklaw (Burnley); Davie Provan (Rangers), Eddie McCreadie (Chelsea); Bobby

Murdoch (Celtic), Ronnie McKinnon (Rangers), John Greig (Rangers); Jim Forrest (Rangers), Billy Bremner (Leeds Utd), Ron Yeats (Liverpool), Charlie Cooke (Dundee), John Hughes (Celtic).

- A fierce competitor in a dark blue jersey, Denis Law famously absented himself from not only England's Wembley final, but from any television screen lest he catch sight of an England victory. Depending on which version of the tale is being related, between the hours of 3.00pm and 5.30pm on 30 July 1966 you can place The Lawman either on the golf course or out walking his dog.

1970 – Mexico

Finished second to West Germany. Having held the Germans 1-1 in Glasgow, and enjoyed 5-0 and 8-0 canters against Cyprus, Scotland went down 3-2 in Hamburg to give Gerd Müller and co. the group. The campaign fizzled out with a 2-0 defeat in Vienna to Austria.

The XI that went down to West Germany – with goals from Johnstone and Gilzean was: Jim Herriot (Birmingham City); John Greig (Rangers), Tommy Gemmell (Celtic); Billy Bremner (Leeds Utd), Ronnie McKinnon (Rangers), Billy McNeill (Celtic); Jimmy Johnstone (Celtic), Peter Cormack (Hibernian), Colin Stein (Rangers), Alan Gilzean (Tottenham Hotspur), Eddie Gray (Leeds Utd).

1994 – United States

Following 0-0 draws against Portugal and Italy in Glasgow, 5-0 and 3-1 drubbings against the same opposition away from home ultimately did for qualification hopes. Slumped to 4th behind Switzerland.

- With Hampden under redevelopment, Scotland's home matches were staged at Ibrox and Pittodrie.

2002 – South Korea & Japan

A draw-heavy campaign, coupled with a scant 2-0 away victory over San Marino – Scotland were held at 0-0 for 70 minutes before Matt Elliott broke the deadlock – saw Scotland fall behind Croatia and Belgium. The 1-1 draw with Croatia took place on the 11 October 2000, the same day that Scotland's First Minister Donald Dewar died.

2006 – Germany

Finished five points adrift of second placed Norway in qualifying, with Italy leading the section. Manager Berti Vogts resigned after three games without a win – including a 1-1 draw with Moldova. Walter Smith's first match in charge was a 2-0 reverse in Milan in March 2005. By September of that year Smith's Scotland were able to hold the Italians 1-1 at Hampden, and were unlucky not to win, but a 1-0 home defeat from Belarus a month later ultimately sunk qualification hopes for the second time in a row.

11 Scotland Greats who Never Graced the World Cup Stage

Jimmy Johnstone (Celtic)*
Ian St John (Motherwell & Liverpool)
Ronnie Simpson (Newcastle Utd, Hibernian & Celtic)
Billy McNeill (Celtic)
John Greig (Rangers)
Jim Baxter (Rangers & Sunderland)
Alan Gilzean (Dundee & Tottenham Hotspur)
Gordon Smith (Hibernian, Hearts & Dundee)
Jimmy McGrory (Celtic)
George Young (Rangers)
Willie Bauld (Hearts)

*Johnstone made the 1974 World Cup squad but featured only on the bench.

The Old Firm

"It takes two, baby"
Marvin Gaye & Kim Weston

Origins of the name "Old Firm"

- As a pejorative term, it implies that the two sides are one clandestine organisation running the game to suit their own ends outside the remit of the Scottish Football Association.
- As a satirical term, it refers to the suspicion that, in the early days, the two clubs would engineer as many money-spinning ties against each other as possible.

≋

Other famous duopolies

Oxford and Cambridge boat race.
The Uppies and the Doonies of Kirkwall, in the Orkney ba game.

≋

Old Firm Managerial Merry-go-Round

Between the 1890 and 1978, 10 men managed the Old Firm. Between 1978 and the present day, 19 individuals have all put in tentative orders for business cards….

≋

Number of Celtic managers from 1897 to 1978 – 4
Jock Stein, Jimmy McGrory, Jimmy McStay and Willie Maley

Number of Rangers managers from 1899 to 1978 – 6

Jock Wallace, Willie Waddell, David White, Scott Symon, William Struth and William Wilton

Number of Celtic managers from 1978 to the present day –12

Gordon Strachan, Martin O'Neill, Kenny Dalglish, John Barnes, Jozef Venglos, Wim Jansen, Tommy Burns, Lou Macari, Liam Brady, Billy McNeill (Twice) and David Hay

Number of Rangers managers from 1978 to the present day – 7

Paul Le Guen, Alex McLeish, Dick Advocaat, Walter Smith, Graeme Souness, Jock Wallace and John Greig

≈≈≈

How Low Can You go?

Old Firm's lowest ever League finishes
Celtic 12th 1947/48
Rangers 6th 1925/26

≈≈≈

Players who have played for both halves of the Old Firm

Alfie Conn (Rangers 1968 – 1974,
Celtic 1977 – 1980)*
Maurice Johnston (Celtic 1984 – 1987,
Rangers 1989 – 1991)
Kenny Miller (Rangers 2000 – 2001,
signed for Celtic 2006)

*Alfie Conn won Scottish Cup medals with both sides: Rangers in 1973, Celtic in 1977.

Only one set of brothers has lined up against each other in an Old Firm match. Tom and Colin MacAdam played for Celtic and Rangers respectively for the first time on 23 August 1980, Rangers winning 2-1 at Celtic Park.

≈≈

Berwick Rangers 1 Rangers 0

Goal: Sammy Reid 23 mins
Shielfield Park, Berwick-upon-Tweed
Scottish Cup First Round
28 January 1967

"That Defeat Will Cost Rangers £100,000."
Sunday Mail front page headline 29 January 1967

"We will come out fighting. There will be no surrender."
Jock Wallace, 31-year-old player-manager of Berwick Rangers in the *Sunday Mail* one week before the match.
"I don't want to detract from the success of Berwick but we had too many bad players in this game."
Rangers manager Scot Symon.

"I am extremely disappointed with the result. Extremely disappointed."
Rangers chairman John Lawrence.

"I knew we could beat them if we tried hard enough and every player in the team gave best."*
Jock Wallace.

"The worst day of my footballing career."
John Greig.
*The *Sunday Mail* report adds the detail that Wallace spoke the words with tears in his eyes.

- Jim Forrest and George MacLean never again played for the Glasgow side: Forrest was off-loaded to Preston North End for £38,000 with McLean moving to Dundee in exchange for Andy Penman.
- The clubs had finished 29 places apart in season 1965/66.
- The Berwick goalscorer that day, Sammy Reid, had been one of Bill Shankly's first signings for Liverpool. Reid, a Glasgow man, was given a lift back home on the Rangers' bus after the match.
- In 1963 Rangers had proposed a restructuring of the Scottish League that would have necessitated the expulsion of Berwick Rangers.

Berwick Rangers: Wallace; Haig, Riddell, Craig, Coutts, Kilgannon, Lumsden, Reid, Christie, Dowds, Ainslie.

Rangers: Martin; Johansen, Provan, Greig, McKinnon, D. Smith, Henderson, A. Smith, McLean, Forrest, Johnston.

- Rangers manager Scot Symon departed the following season – the first manager in Rangers' history to be sacked – in November. His Rangers side were top of the League, one point clear of Celtic.

Celtic 1 Inverness Caledonian Thistle 3

Scorers: Celtic – Mark Burchill (17 mins);
Inverness Barry Wilson (16 mins), Lubomir Moravcik
(og 24 mins), Paul Sheerin (pen 55 mins)
Scottish Cup Third Round
8 February 2000

"Humiliation for Celtic in shock cup exit".
The Scotsman front page headline 9 February 2000.

"We have no need to be in awe of Celtic. We are a half-decent side and if we play to our potential we can give them a game".
Steve Paterson, ICT manager, in the *Daily Record*
before the match.

"To be honest, if the situation does not improve by the end of the season, I won't have to consider my situation, it will be done for me".
Celtic manager John Barnes on the Cup exit and being 10 points behind Rangers.

"Totally unacceptable to myself and my fellow directors. Not good enough for the support".
Celtic Chief-Executive Allan MacDonald.

"The worst Celtic result ever without a doubt. What was surprising was not the defeat but the ease with which the defeat was accomplished, and the margin".
Bob Crampsey, writer and author of Celtic's Centenary history.

"If you don't want to wear the Celtic jersey, then don't turn up for work tomorrow".
Kenny Dalglish's warning to his new charges as he takes over the reins as Celtic manager.

"They (the Celtic players) will live with this for the rest of their lives".

Kai Johansen, survivor of Rangers' defeat at Berwick in the pages of the *Daily Record*.

- The initial tie on the 30th January had been called off at the last minute due to loose guttering on the roof of the newly christened Lisbon Lions Stand. Upon hearing the announcement while travelling to the game, billed on the radio as "shock news from Parkhead", ICT boss Steve Paterson remarked, "I thought they had sacked John Barnes".
- The clubs had finished 19 places apart in season 1998/99.
- The ICT goalkeeper on the night was 39-year-old Jim Calder, a builder by trade.
- The Celtic XI that night had been assembled at the cost of £20m. ICT had splashed out £50,000. Celtic's share price slumped by an estimated £3m the next morning.

Inverness Caledonian Thistle: Calder; Michael Teasdale, Stuart Golabek, Bobby Mann, Richard Hastings, Paul Sheerin, Ross Tokely, Mark McCulloch, Charlie Christie, Barry Wilson, Dennis Wyness.

Celtic: Jonathan Gould; Tommy Boyd, Olivier Tebily, Stephane Mahe, Vidar Riseth, Colin Healy, Regi Blinker, Lubomir Moravcik, Eyal Berkovic, Mark Viduka (Ian Wright 46), Mark Burchill.

- Of the 14 outfield players deployed by John Barnes on the night of the 8 February 2000, only one – Colin Healy – started the match under Martin O'Neill on the day that Celtic lifted the league flag in 2001. A further two – Tom Boyd and Lubomir Moravcik – participated as substitutes.

- Celtic manager John Barnes was sacked within 48 hours of the defeat and with him went assistant manager Eric Black and coach Terry McDermott.
- Fergus Ewing, the Scottish Nationalist MSP for Inverness East, Nairn and Lochaber wasted no time in gaining political capital from the result, tabling the following motion: *"That the Parliament hopes that the historic victory of Inverness Caledonian Thistle over Celtic on 8 February 2000 will be followed by success for Inverness in being awarded City status, which as a premier football location in Scotland it surely deserves"*.

≈≈

Potless

Old Firm managers who didn't need to remember to pack their mementoes of cup wins when clearing their desks:

David White – Rangers 1967 to 1969*.
Liam Brady Celtic 1991 to 1993#
Lou Macari Celtic 1993 to 1994#
Josef Venglos Celtic 1998 to 1999*
John Barnes – Celtic 1999 to 2000#

*Led their respective teams to defeat against Old Firm rivals in Scottish Cup Final.

Did not reach a major final.

≈≈

Only two managers have left the hot seats at the Old Firm and gone on to win trophies at another Scottish Club: Rangers' David White (the League Cup with Dundee in 1973/74) and Celtic's David Hay (the League Cup with Livingston in 2003/04).

Europe

"We cannae play these defensive continental sides."
*Liverpool manager Bill Shankly following his team's 5-1
reverse at the hands of Ajax in Amsterdam, European Cup
1966/67*

Scottish Clubs in Europe

European Cup

Winners: Celtic 1966/67
Runner-up: Celtic 1969/70
Semi-finalists: Celtic 1971/72, 1973/74; Dundee
1962/63; Dundee Utd 1983/84; Hibernian 1955/56;
Rangers 1959/60, 1992/93*
Quarter-finalists: Aberdeen 1985/86; Celtic 1968/69,
1970/71, 1979,80; Rangers 1961/62, 1964/65, 1987/88
*Group match, essentially a semi-final. Tournament
now called the UEFA Champions' League

European Cup Winners' Cup

Winners: Aberdeen 1982/83; Rangers 1971/72
Runner-up: Rangers 1960/61, 1966/67
Semi-finalists: Aberdeen 1983/84; Celtic 1963/64,
1965/66; Dunfermline 1968/69
Quarter-finalists: Celtic 1975/76; Dunfermline 1961/62;
Hibernian 1972/73; Rangers 1978/79

UEFA/Fairs Cup

Runner-up: Celtic 2002/03; Dundee Utd 1986/87
Semi-finalists: Kilmarnock 1966/67; Dundee 1967/68
Quarter-finalists: Dunfermline 1965/66; Dundee Utd

1981/82, 1982/83; Hearts 1988/89; Hibernian 1960/61; Rangers 1967/68, 1968/69

- For the 15 year period from season 1959/60 to season 1973/74, Scotland had at least one side every year in the last eight of European competition.

≈≈

17 Scottish clubs have competed in European competition.

They are:

Aberdeen
Airdrieonians
Celtic
Dundee
Dundee Utd
Dunfermline Athletic
Greenock Morton
Gretna
Hearts
Hibernian
Kilmarnock
Livingston
Partick Thistle
Raith Rovers
Rangers
St Johnstone
St Mirren

- Germany, Spain, Italy and England are the unhappiest hunting grounds where 35, 25, 23 and 19 ties respectively have been lost to the end of season 2005/06.

- Highest scoring single European tie: Aberdeen 10 KR Reykjavik (Iceland) 1, Cup Winners' Cup First Round 1967/68, Dunfermline 10 Apoel (Cyprus) 1, Cup Winners' Cup First Round 1968/69.
- Highest aggregate score 14-2, Aberdeen v. KR Reykjavik (Iceland) Cup Winners' Cup First Round 1967/68.
- With 3-0 home win over Benfica being followed by a 0-3 reverse in Portugal, Celtic progressed to the quarter-finals of the 1969/70 European Cup on the toss of a coin.
- Rangers are one of the five sides to have won the old European Cup Winners' Cup despite not having won their domestic cup to qualify for the tournament (they lost 1971's replayed final 2-1 to Celtic). The others are Fiorentina (1960/61), Anderlecht (1977/78), Dynamo Tblisi (1980/81) and Barcelona (1996/97).

Scots with European Cup winners' medals:

Ronnie Simpson (Celtic)
Jim Craig (Celtic)
Tommy Gemmell (Celtic)
Bobby Murdoch (Celtic)
Billy McNeill (Celtic)
John Clark (Celtic)
Jimmy Johnstone (Celtic)
William Wallace (Celtic)
Stevie Chalmers (Celtic)
Bertie Auld (Celtic)
Bobby Lennox (Celtic)
Pat Crerand (Manchester United)
Alan Hansen (Liverpool)
Graeme Souness (Liverpool)
Kenny Dalglish (Liverpool)

John McGovern (Nottingham Forest)
Kenny Burns (Nottingham Forest)
John Robertson (Nottingham Forest)
Des Bremner (Aston Villa)
Stevie Nicol (Liverpool)
Paul Lambert (Borussia Dortmund)
Alex Ferguson (Manchester United)*
Alex Miller (Liverpool)#

*As manager – a distinction unavailable to Jock Stein in 1967 or Matt Busby in 1968;# As assistant manager. NB Archie Gemmill was dropped for Nottingham Forest's 1979 European Cup final. Denis Law was invalided out of the 1968 European Cup final.

≈≈≈

Scots to win the Golden Boot*

1991/92 Ally McCoist – Rangers – 34 goals
1992/93 Ally McCoist – Rangers – 34 goals

*Although no Golden Boot was officially awarded from 1991/92 until 1995/96, the title is still commonly used to refer to Europe's top scorers of the period.

≈≈≈

Scots to have won European Player of the Year

1964 – Denis Law (Manchester United)

≈≈≈

Winners of the Golden Boot whilst playing for Scottish Clubs

2000/01 Henrik Larsson – Celtic – 35 goals

- Only four European cities can boast two European finalists in one season. Glasgow is one of those cities, with Celtic and Rangers reaching the finals of the 1966/67 European Cup and European Cup Winners' Cup respectively. (The other cities are Madrid 61/62 & 85/86, Liverpool 84/85 and Milan 93/94).
- Two Scottish cities have sent two sides to the semi-final of the European Cup – Glasgow and Dundee. They share this distinction with nine other European cities: Belgrade, Bucharest, Budapest, London, Madrid, Milan, Moscow, Prague and Vienna.

~~~

Consecutive Qualifications for Europe

26 Rangers (1981/82 – 2006/07)
16 Celtic (1962/63 – 1977/78)
15 Aberdeen (1977/78 – 1991/92)

~~~

Scotland's most successful season in Europe: 1966/67

Scotland sent a team to the semi-final of each of the three major European trophies – Celtic, Rangers and Kilmarnock

European Cup Final Celtic 2 Internazionale 1
European Cup Winners' Cup Final Bayern Munich 1 Rangers 0
Fairs Cup semi-final Kilmarnock 2 Leeds United 4 (agg)

All Over the Place at the Back.

What a Stramash*!

A gallimaufry within a gallimaufry

Stramash: a noun favoured by Scottish football commentators, defined in Chambers Scots Dictionary as an uproar; a commotion or tumult. It enjoys a particular association with legendary STV commentator Arthur Montford

≈≈

Who Ate All the Pies?# 1

Don't just sit there mumpin about the quality of away pies: make your own. To make four pies you will need:

450g of lean minced lamb or mutton
800g hot water crust pastry (see Who Ate All the Pies#2)
1 tsp Worcestershire sauce
1 small onion, minced
4 tbsp of beef stock
Salt & pepper to taste

Rock'n'Roll Ain't Noise Pollution

In September 1989, Terry Butcher confessed his all-time top ten songs to *Shoot!* comic:

Wasted Years – Iron Maiden.
Fly on the Wall – AC/DC
Bad Medicine – Bon Jovi
Empty Rooms – Gary Moore
Number of the Beast – Iron Maiden
Sebastian – Steve Harley & Cockney Rebel
Paradise City – Guns n Roses
Dallas 1pm – Saxon
The Clairvoyant – Iron Maiden
Overkill – Motörhead

≈

Firsts Among Equals

When times are hard and trophies few, nostalgia and statistics become the currency. Here are a few firsts boasted by Scottish clubs and their fans in lieu of silverware in those difficult, cup-hungry years.

World's First Dugout – Aberdeen
First All-Seater Stadium in Scotland – Aberdeen
First Club Newspaper – Celtic
First Winner of the FIFA Fair Play Award – Dundee Utd
First Scottish Team in Europe – Hibernian
First Club in Scotland – Queen's Park

The Tunnock's Tea Cakes Shield

The open-top bus may have remained in the garage, but glory-hungry fans and clubs still claim bragging rights. Try....

Pie of the Year 1996 – Kilmarnock FC
Programme of the Year 1974/75, 1977/78, 1978/79, 1981/82* – Hamilton Academicals
Airdrie Charities Cup 1891/92 – Albion Rovers
Champions of the World 1887 – Hibernian
Third Place in Scottish League 1947/48; 1953/54; 1962/63*– Partick Thistle
*Source: Fans' entry in the online encyclopaedia Wikipdepia

≈

I Write the Songs That Make the Whole World Sing

Some football chants and songs and their origins.

The Celtic Song (For It's a Grand Old Team to Play For)
Origin: Operetta.
The Pirates of Penzance, music by Arthur Sullivan, words by William Gilbert, 1879. Later adapted as the vaudeville song *Hail! Hail! The Gang's All Here* (1917, words by DA Estron).

Hearts, Hearts, Glorious Hearts
Origin: Comic song *The Hippopotamus* written by Michael Flanders & Donald Swann 1959. Commonly known as *Mud, Mud Glorious Mud*.

One Paddy Stanton! There's Only One Paddy Stanton! (*Vide* Henry Hall, Andy Ritchie, et al)

Origin: Calypso/Protest. *Guantanamera*, original music by Jose Fernandez Diaz, music adaptation by Pete Seeger & Julian Orbon, lyric adaptation by Julian Orbon, based on a patriotic Cuban poem by Jose Marti.

Hello! Hello! We are the Billy Boys

Origin: Marching song of the American Civil War entitled *Marching Through Georgia* composed by Henry Clay Work 1865. Was also adopted as the anthem of the Liberal Party as the protest song *The Land*.

We Hate Jimmy Hill

Origin: 70s/80s Advertising campaign.

Fly the Flag, BA ad campaign, later used as the B-side to the 1982 England World Cup Squad's hit *This Time (We'll Get it Right)*.

We Are (Insert team here) FC./We hate Jam Tarts and we hate Dundee

Origin: Hymn.

Based on the Shaker hymn/work song *Simple Gifts*, composed by Joseph Brackett in 1797. Adapted in 1963 as *The Lord of the Dance* by Sydney Carter.

Ooh to be a Hibbie

Origin: Early 60s pop music.

Based on one of the first ever football chants, from the Kop at Anfield, where the fans adapted the rhythmic Chants hit *Let's Go!*, replacing the "Let's go!" refrain with the surname of their Scottish centre-forward, Ian St John.

We'd Walk a Million Miles for One of Your Goals

Origin: Hollywood musical.

My Mammy, written by Walter Donaldson for the 1930 movie *Mammy*, starring Al Jolson. Other

Donaldson hits include *My Blue Heaven*, a favourite of sub-editors writing headlines on upbeat Rangers stories.

You'll Never Walk Alone*

Origin: Musical theatre.

Written by Richard Rodgers and Oscar Hammerstein II for the Broadway musical *Carousel* in 1945. Rodgers and Hammerstein also composed Tartan Army fave *Do-Re-Mi* for their show *The Sound of Music*.

*Originally adopted by Liverpool FC supporters in 1963, following the chart success of Liverpool fan Gerry Marsden's version. Later adopted by Celtic and other sides across the globe including Ajax, Feyenoord, FC Twente (all Holland), St Pauli and Borussia Dortmund (Germany) and FC. Tokyo.

≈≈≈

"Oh, mama! Don't Forget to Order Bovril!"*

- Bovril was invented by a Scot, John Lawson Johnston, born in Roslin, Midlothian in 1839.
- Contracted in 1870 by Napoleon III to provide a million cans of beef for the French Army, Johnson developed his "Fluid Beef".
- The name Bovril comes from the Latin for Ox – Bovine – and Vril, an electric fluid that gives super powers to a race of subterranean beings, who subsequently take over the world, in the early science fiction novel *The Coming Race* (1870) by Edward Bulwer-Lytton.
- In 2004, all traces of meat were removed from Bovril, which became a vegetarian-friendly yeast-extract drink.

*Early 20th century advertising campaign slogan

For the Gullible Outsider: The Derbies that are NOT really Derbies

East Fife v. East Stirlingshire
St Johnstone v. St Mirren
(For the European equivalent see Borussia
Dortmund v. Borussia Moenchengladbach)

~~~~~

Most Unlikely Celebrity Fan on the Famous Football Supporters' website

David Byrne of Talking Heads supports Dumbarton. *The Famous Football Supporters' website can be found at www. ffsp.railwayinn.me.uk*

~~~~~

THAT headline

On the morning of the 9 February 2000, the football world awoke to the *Scottish Sun* headline:

Super Caley Go Ballistic, Celtic Are Atrocious
Celtic had lost 3-1 to Division One side Inverness Caledonian Thistle. The glory goes to then-*Sun* Chief Sports Sub Editor Paul Hickson. It is claimed, however, that the headline has two precedents:

Super Caley Are Fantastic, Airdrie Quite Atrocious
From the *Daily Star* following Airdrie's dismissal from the tournament by the old Inverness Caledonian, then of the Highland League; and….

Super Cally Was Fantastic, QPR Atrocious
Which was how the *Liverpool Echo* saluted a memorable performance from Reds' legend Ian Callaghan against the west London side in 1976.

Some Rhyming Slang

Harry Wraggs

Post-war rhyming slang for cigarette: Harry Wragg = fag. Adopted by fans of Partick Thistle to rhyme also with Jags. The real Harry Wragg was the Champion jockey in 1941 and in his career was a winner of The Oaks, The St Leger and The Derby.

Willie Bauld

In Edinburgh and surrounding environs, gentlemen of a certain age will still refer to a brisk morning as being a bit Willie Bauld – i.e. "cauld" – after the great Hearts forward of the 1950s.

Glasgow Rangers

Cockney rhyming slang coinage circ. 2000. East London parlance for a gathering of unfamiliar people: Glasgow Rangers = strangers.

≈≈≈

Who Ate All the Pies?# 2

The Pastry

170g of plain flour.

170 ml of water.

85g of lard.

Pinch of salt.

Sift flour and salt in a bowl. Make a well in the centre.

Put water and lard in a saucepan. Melt the lard, then bring to the boil.

Decant the mixture into the well of the flour. Mix with a wooden spoon, then knead until the dough is smooth.

NB: It is imperative to use the pastry while it is still warm. If not, it will become brittle and too hard to work with and shape.

Playing Away

Scottish League teams who have played competitive football in other countries:

Aberdeen

In the summer of 1967, Aberdeen played in the USA in a forerunner of the North American Soccer League, going by the name of the Washington Whips.

Dundee Utd

Participated in the same fledgling NASL as Aberdeen, under the name of Dallas Tornado.

Berwick Rangers

Famously based over the border in England.

Gretna

Played in England's Northern Premier League until 2002. In the 1990s they became the first Scottish club to play in the FA Cup since 1887.

Queen's Park

Reached the semi-final of the FA Cup in 1871/72 and 1872/73. This achievement was subsequently matched by....

Rangers

Reached the semi-final of the FA Cup in 1886/87, losing 3-1 to Aston Villa.

≈

Clydebank FC was the first Scottish Club to have a computer installed. "It will handle the wages and accounts of the club," Chairman Jack Steadman informed the *Sunday Mail* in November 1980.

Some Scottish Football Nicknames and their Origins

The Loons

Forfar Athletic was founded by the younger second XI breaking away from Angus Athletic. As this XI was comprised of younger men the Loons – Loon meaning boy or young man – became their nickname.

The Doonhamers

Queen of the South fans working away from their home town traditionally referred to Dumfries as Doon Hame (down home).

The Bairns

From the old Falkirk burgh motto: "Better meddle wi the deil (devil) than the bairns o Falkirk".

The Blue Brazil

Satirical monicker linking low-achieving Cowdenbeath (who play in blue strips) to world dominating Brazilian national side. (See also Maryhill Magyars).

The Arabs

Legend has it that Dundee Utd's pitch was so bare during the winter of 1962/63 that a lorry load of sand was spread over its surface for a cup-tie against Albion Rovers. This desert-like surface inspired the nickname.

Montford's Mad Movies

Due to the cumbersome nature of early TV cameras, and their inability to swivel and pan to catch deflected shots, much TV coverage was rendered nonsensical to the viewer. The unflattering nickname comes from the *Scotsport* presenter of the day, Arthur Montford.

In Focus…

During the 1970s and 1980s the football comic *Shoot!* ran a weekly series of Q&A interviews with major soccer stars. In 1976, Tommy Docherty was In Focus…

Tommy Docherty (Manchester United)
Q: Which person in the world would you most like to meet?
A: "I've met him – The Pope"
Q: Second choice? A: "Perry Como"

≈

Jimmy Hill: Verbatim

Since 1982, English TV pundit Jimmy Hill has been persona non grata with the Tartan Army for perceived derogatory remarks made in his TV analysis of David Narey's wonder goal that opened – and closed – Scotland's account against Brazil in their Group F encounter*. Hill's full quote, however, reveals a more even-handed, dare it be said even pro-Scotland sentiment:

"If you wanted to be rude you could call it a toe-poke, if you wanted to be kind you could call it an exhilarating Brazilian skill, but what matters is, it went in"#.

The Tartan Army can, of course, feel free to insinuate that Mr Hill's Johnsonian anti-Scottishness was implied in his tone.

*Narey's team mate Gordon Strachan later suggested that the goal – a 35 yard strike – merely had the effect of riling the Brazilians, akin to poking a stick in a wasps' nest. Brazil ran out 4-1 winners.

Wick Academy is Britain's northernmost senior football team.

Ex-Rangers player Albert Gudmundsson ran for President of Iceland in 1980.

Who Ate All the Pies?# 3

Method:
Preheat oven to 120°C/Gas Mark 1.
Grease (lightly) the outer sides and base of four jam jars and a baking sheet.
Set aside one quarter of the pastry for the lids. Important: keep it warm.
Divide the remaining pastry into four. Again, keep it warm.
Press one portion of the pastry into a circle and place over the upturned jam jar. Keep it even, letting it reach roughly 5 cms up the side of the jar. Keep it an even thickness of 1 cm. Set aside to cool and repeat with the other jars.
Cut some greaseproof paper the same depth as that of the pastry case and long enough to wrap around the case, securing it with string.
Place the upturned jar on to the baking sheet and carefully remove the pastry case.
Mix all of the filling ingredients together and divide the mixture between the pastry cases.
Trim the pastry case to the level of the meat.
Shape the remaining pastry into a round lid for the pie.
Moisten the edges and crimp to seal the pie. Glaze with beaten egg (using a brush).
Make a hole in the centre, to allow steam to escape.
Bake for 45 minutes or until lightly golden

Take this Cup Away From Me...

Some defunct trophies.

The Texaco Cup

Tourney that ran from 1971 – 1975 for English, Scottish and (until 1973/74) Irish clubs that had not qualified for Europe. Hearts lost the two-legged final 3-2 to Wolves in the inaugural year with Airdrieonians going down to Derby County the following season. Became the Anglo-Scottish Cup when Texaco withdrew their sponsorship.

The Anglo-Scottish Cup

Essentially the same tournament as the Texaco Cup, sans the multinational sponsorship deal, St Mirren were the only Scottish winners of the trophy, beating Bristol City 5-1 in the 1980 final (the Buddies had lost to the same opposition in the 1978 final by 3-2). Is perhaps best remembered for Rangers' 4-1 humiliation at the hands of lowly Chesterfield in 1981 – the last year Scottish clubs took part.

The European Cup Winners' Cup

With two wins (Rangers in 1972 and Aberdeen in 1983 defeating Real Madrid in the final) Scotland's favourite European trophy in terms of success. Rangers made an additional two finals (losing in 1961 and 1967). Celtic made the semi-finals in 1964 and 1974 as did Dunfermline in 1968.

The Coronation Cup

A one off football tournament contested between four English – Arsenal, Manchester United, Newcastle and Tottenham Hotspur – and four Scottish – Aberdeen, Celtic, Hibernian and Rangers – clubs to celebrate the coronation of Queen Elizabeth II. The knockout cup was rather dominated by the north-of-the-border sides.

Celtic won the final 2-0, beating Hibs before 117,06 spectators at Hampden.

The Rous Cup

International trophy contested in 1985 and 1986 between Scotland and England, and then from 1987 – 1989 between those two and a South American guest – Brazil in 1987, Colombia in 1988 and Chile in 1989. Scotland lifted the trophy only once, in 1985 after a 1-0 win over England at Hampden thanks to a Richard Gough header.

In the Pokey

They're coming home they've done their time….

Duncan Ferguson

Served six weeks in HMP Barlinnie in 1996 (by which
time he was an Everton player) for head-butting Raith
Rovers' John McStay while playing for Rangers.

George Best

Four years after leaving Hibs in 1984, Best served
three months for drink driving, assaulting a police
officer and failing to answer bail. Turned out for the
Ford Open Prison XI.

Olivier Tebily

In what may have been the most chaotic week in the
history of Celtic Football Club, in the run up to the
Cup defeat against Inverness, Ivory Coast full-back
Oliver Tebily was held against his will along with his
team mates for 48 hours of intensive training at an
army detention camp following an early exit from the
African Nations' Cup.

❖ ❖ ❖

The first live TV broadcast of a game in Scotland,
on 23 April 1955, was the Scottish Cup Final between
Clyde and Celtic. It was a 0-0 draw. Rather than use
a Scottish commentator, Kenneth Wolstenholme was
flown up from London specially for the occasion.

Stick 'em Up

The Figurine Panini sticker albums that have accompanied the World Cup Finals every year from 1970 acted not only as a hobby for football daft kids, but in 1974 functioned as every Scottish child's first introduction to foreign languages. Fantasies of fluent discourse with fans of all nations were fuelled with German, French, Italian, Dutch and Spanish translations for the following words and phrases:

Scotland: Schottland; Ecosse; Scozia; Schotland; Escocia.

"How they Qualified": Hat sich so gualifiziert; S'est qualiifiée comme suit; Si e qualificata cosí; Kwalificeerde zich als volgt; Se ha calificado así.

Goalkeeper: Torthüter; Gardien de but ; Portiere; Keeper; Potero.

Full-back: Abwehrspieler; Arriere; Difensore; Verdediger; Defensor.

Half-back: Mittelfeldspieler; Mileu; Centrocampista; MiddenveldsPelér; Medio campista.

Forward: Stürmer; Avant; Attacc; Aanvaller; Delantero.

"Final Positions": Endstand; Classement final; Classifica finale; Eindclassificatie; Clasificacion.

- By Italia '90, the wealth of trivial information contained in the pages of the sticker books comprised not only date and place of birth, club side and position, but also the height and weight of each squad member. Alan McInally was purported to be the heaviest member of the squad at 85 kg; Dave McPherson the tallest at 1.90m; Paul McStay the lightest at 67 kg; and Stuart McCall the smallest at 1.69m.

- Often printed ahead of the squad announcement, the collections sometimes featured players who didn't make the tournament. Kenny Dalglish features in the Mexico '86 album although he had to pull out through injury. And the 1978 album achieves what Ally MacLeod failed to do and includes Andy Gray in the squad.

Alliteration in Scottish Fitba

The heart-quickening linguistic tic that is alliteration is defined by the OED thus: **alliteration** *n.* the occurrence of the same latter or sound at the beginning of adjacent or closely connected words (e.g. *cool, calm and collected*).

Over the years, Scots sportswriters have proved to be adroit practitioners of the art, adding (among many others) the following names and phrases to the Scottish fitba lexicon.

The Maryhill Magyars

Coined by a Glasgow *Evening Times* scribe for an attractive Partick Thistle side of the '50s – Maryhill is the burgh in which the team plays, the Magyars an allusion to the world-beating Hungarian national side of the '50s (the Hungarian for Hungary is Magyarország).

The Wembley Wizards

The side that destroyed England 5-1 at Wembley in 1928 (Harkness, Nelson, Law, Gibson, Bradshaw, McMullan, Jackson, Dunn, Gallacher, James, Morton). In a characteristically Scottish season, this ritual humiliation of the next-door neighbours in their own back garden lifted Scotland to a mere third in that year's Home International Championship.

The Famous Five

The Hibs forward line of the '50s – Gordon Smith, Bobby Johnstone, Eddie Turnbull, Lawrie Reilly and Willie Ormond. This legendary line won three League Championships

The Terrible Trio

Not to be outdone, the other side of Edinburgh offered their own alliterative forward threesome of the 1950s – Jimmy Wardhaugh, Willie Bauld and Alfie Conn. Thanks to their services, Hearts won two League Championships, a League Cup and a Scottish Cup.

The Blue Brazil

Alliteration seemed to catch on among supporters, and is exemplified in perhaps the best of all Scottish Club nicknames – Cowdenbeath's The Blue Brazil, a factual reference to the light blue shirts of the Fifers, and a deeply ironic and self-effacing comparison between the Scottish underachievers and the planet's most successful national side.

≈≈≈

The Hair Bear Bunch

Some Rangers players with noteworthy hair.

Derek Johnstone – perm and beard combo graced the bench at Argentina '78.

Graeme Souness – the most imposing moustache in world football.

John Greig – bearded for the Cup Winners' Cup win to hide a scar on his chin.

Alfie Conn – the sideburns that ate New York.

Lorenzo Amoruso – 'do like a cavalier football side: tidy up front, a disaster at the back.

Paul Gascoigne – bottle blond bombshell.

Claudio Canigia – head band or head banned?

Scottish Football Grounds Named after Englishmen

Hampden Park (Queen's Park)
Named for nearby street Hampden Terrace, which in turn takes its title from an English politician and patriot killed in 1643 during the English Civil War.

Palmerston Park (Queen of the South)
Henry Templeton, 3rd Viscount Palmerston, Prime Minister of Great Britain 1855 – 1858, 1859 – 1865.

~~~

It's Wee, It's Red, and It's a Book

That essential piece of supporters' kit, the *Wee Red Book* – its full, original title being *The Evening Times Football Annual* – was first printed in 1928.

Hampden Park

Until 1950 and the creation of the Maracaña in Brazil, Hampden Park was the largest football stadium in the world, and still boasts each and every major European attendance record: International – 149,547, Scotland v. England, 1937; Domestic – 146,433, Celtic v. Aberdeen, Scottish Cup 1937; and European club – 136,505 : Celtic v. Leeds United, European Cup semi-final 1970. Football firsts at Hampden include:

First turnstiles.
First press box (added 1906)
First public address system
First car park
The first all-ticket match 1884

NB: The first ever international match – a nil-nil draw between Scotland and England in 1872 – although staged in Glasgow, did not take place at Hampden Park, but at the West of Scotland Cricket Ground.

~~~

The European Cup Final 1960

Widely regarded as the greatest European Cup Final of them all, Real Madrid beat Eintracht Frankfurt 7 – 3 at Hampden Park on 18 May 1960 to win the trophy for the 5th time in front of 135,000 – largely local – fans.

• Finalists Eintracht Frankfurt had beaten Rangers 6-1 in Frankfurt and 6-3 at Ibrox in the semi-final.

• The only Scot on the park was respected referee John A. Mowatt. Many years later, Mr Mowatt joked to the *Daily Record* that he had claimed expenses for a train journey to the match, even though he had walked most of the way, thus fiddling Europe's soccer mandarins out of the princely sum of sixpence*.

The Teams

Real Madrid Rogelio Antonio Domínguez; Marquitos, José Emilio Santamaría, Pachin, José María Vidal, José María Zárraga (Captain); Canario, Luis del Sol, Alfredo di Stefano, Ferenc Puskas, Francisco Gento

Eintracht Frankfurt

Egon Loy; Friedel Lutz, Hermann Höfer; Hans Weilbächer (Captain), Hans-Walter Eigenbrodt, Dieter Stinka; Richard Kreß, Dieter Lindner, Erwin Stein, Alfred Pfaff, Erich Meier Trainer: Paul Oßwald

The scorers

Real Madrid	**Eintracht Frankfurt**.
Alfredo di Stefano (27)	Richard Kreß (18)
Alfredo di Stefano (30)	Erwin Stein (72)
Ferenc Puskas (46)	Erwin Stein (75)
Ferenc Puskas (56)	
Ferenc Puskas (60)	
Ferenc Puskas (71)	
Alfredo di Stefano (73)	

*Two years earlier, Mr Mowatt had become the oldest referee at the World Cup, officiating in Hungary's 4-0 rout of Mexico on 15 June 1958 at the age of 50.

≈≈

In addition to his 22 Scotland football caps (all earned while with Liverpool), Alan Hansen has also represented Scotland at squash, volleyball and golf, all at Under-18 level.

Teams that have yet to send a player on Scottish international duty

Airdrie United
Berwick Rangers
Elgin City
Forfar Athletic
Gretna
Livingston
Peterhead
Ross County
Stenhousemuir
Stirling Albion
Stranraer

How to get up the nose of a serious football trivia buff in six easy steps

1. Say: "I've got one for you. You'll never get it.".
2. When your subject protests, say: "It's hard, mind.".
3. After some protest, acquiesce, with the following caveat: "Okay… but no clues, you'll get it far too quickly with an in-depth knowledge like yours.".
4. Pose the question: "Who played football for Scotland and Cricket for England?".
5. Beat off all requests for clues*.
6. Provide the answer as: Geoff Boycott and Denis Law or Andrew Flintoff and Barry Ferguson or Mike Gatting and Kenny Dalglish – any combination of English cricketer and Scottish footballer.

*(*If you must give a clue, state that it was neither Andy Goram nor Scot Symon, who both played cricket for Scotland, nor Ian Botham who played cricket for England and club football with Scunthorpe United)*

Other football books from SportsBooks

Wembley – The Complete Record 1923–2000

Every football match ever played at the world's most iconic football stadium is detailed in this exhaustive reference work. Paperback. ISBN 1899807 42 X £14.99

≈≈

Ha'Way/Howay the Lads

A history of the rivalry between Newcastle United and Sunderland. Paperback. ISBN 1899807 39 X £14.99

≈≈

Ode to Jol

A sideways, and very funny, look at Tottenham Hotspurs' 2005/06 season. Paperback. ISBN 1899807 43 8 £12.99

≈≈

Accrington Stanley - the club that wouldn't die

Accrington Stanley returned to the Football League this year after resigning in 1962. This tells the story of the years of struggle and eventual triumph. Hardback. ISBN 1899807 47 0 £16.99

Black Lions - a history of black players in English football

The story of black players in English football, with interviews with players such as Garth Crooks, John Barnes and Luther Blissett. Hardback. ISBN 1899807 38 1 £16.99

~~~

Harry Potts – Margaret's Story

Harry Potts was Burnley's manager in the days the small-town team won the league and reached the FA Cup final. This is his story told by his widow Margaret and Dave Thomas. Great photographic section. Hardback. ISBN 1899807 41 1 £17.99

~~~

Growing up with Subbuteo – my dad invented the world's greatest football game

Mark Adolph tells the story of growing up with his father Peter, the man who invented Subbuteo. A very funny, often poignant account of life with an eccentric father. Paperback. ISBN 1899807 40 3 £7.99

~~~

Europe United – a history of the European Cup/Champions League

The enthralling story of the European Cup/Champions League. Hardback. ISBN 1899807 30 6 £17.99

~~~

Raich Carter – the biography

The only man to win an FA Cup winners' medal before and after the war and the man England preferred to partner Stanley Matthews. Hardback. ISBN 1899807 18 7 £16.99

≈≈

The Complete Centre-Foward – a biography of Tommy Lawton

Another player who had his career interrupted by the Second World War, Lawton caused a huge shock when he moved from First Division Chelsea to Notts County from the Third Division, a little like Michael Owen moving to, well, Notts County now. Hardback. ISBN 1899807 09 8 £14.99